Snowboarding

Snowboarding

Greg Goldman

NEW
HOLLAND

NEW
HOLLAND

First published in 2001
This edition published in 2009 by
New Holland Publishers Ltd
London • Cape Town • Sydney • Auckland
www.newhollandpublishers.com

86-88 Edgware Road
London W2 2EA
United Kingdom

80 McKenzie Street
Cape Town 8001
South Africa

Unit 1, 66 Gibbes Street
Chatswood, NSW 2067
Australia

218 Lake Road
Northcote, Auckland
New Zealand

Copyright © 2009, 2001 New Holland Publishers (UK) Ltd
Copyright © 2009, 2001 in text: Greg Goldman
Copyright © 2001 in illustrations: New Holland
Publishers (UK) Ltd
Copyright © 2001 in photographs: All photographs by Miles
Masterson for Struik Image Library (SIL) except the individual
photographers and/or their agents as listed on page 95.

ISBN 978 1 84773 343 6

Publisher: Mariëlle Renssen
Commissioning Editors: Mari Roberts (UK)
Claudia dos Santos (SA)
Managing Art Editor: Peter Bosman
Editors: Lauren Copley, Romi Bryden
Designer: Sonia van Essen
Illustrator: Steven Felmore
Picture researcher: Sonya Meyer
Proofreader: Ingrid Schneider
Production: Myrna Collins
Consultants: Steve Ensor (UK), Axel Zander (SA)

Reproduction by Hirt & Carter (Cape) Pty Ltd
Printed and bound in Singapore by Craft Print (Pte) Ltd

4 6 8 10 9 7 5 3

Disclaimer

This is a handbook on snowboarding skills
should not be used as a substitute for les
taught by a certified professional snowboar
instructor. Nothing in this book should be
as advice to undertake dangerous manoeuvre
to explore uncontrolled environments without
proper guidance and training.

Although the author and publishers have n
every effort to ensure that the informa

contained in this book was accurate at the time of going to press, they accept no responsibility for any accident, loss or inconvenience sustained by any person using this book or the advice given in it.

Author's acknowledgements

Thanks first and foremost to my father, for helping me get the opportunity to write this book and for his advice along the way. Also thanks to the rest of my family for listening, and to Karen, Greg and the Jones Boys for their friendship and guidance. Extra special thanks to Claudia dos Santos and Lauren Copley for their patience and hard work.

Finally, special thanks to the National Ski Patrol for allowing me to leverage their knowledge and experience in reprinting their Responsibility Code and Backcountry Safety Information.

Dedication

For Stephane

Contents

The Sport for All

Who would have thought it possible? A sport that combines the free-flowing, fluid movement of surfing and the aerial activity of skateboarding with the adrenalin rush of high-speed fun and the high-altitude beauty of an alpine environment.

This is snowboarding: the perfect fusion of solitude and exhilaration. Try it once and you will wonder how the world ever got along without it. While other winter recreation sports like skiing originally developed out of necessity, snowboarding developed strictly out of the desire for fun.

The sport has come a long way in its roughly 40 years of existence. Today it's hard to believe that it was once only a barely legitimate winter sport with a small but dedicated band of followers. Even after the early days of backcountry-only riding finally gave way to an era where a few resorts allowed snowboarding access, achieving mainstream acceptance seemed like a far-fetched goal. The relatively sudden explosion of the sport onto the world's resort scene in the 1990s took even snowboarders by surprise, and its growth and popularity has steadily increased over time. It's estimated that over 3.5 million snowboarders now make up about 35 percent of the total winter resort visitors worldwide.

Explosion in Popularity

Winter resorts have embraced this demographic explosion for some time now, and their efforts have allowed the sport to make enormous strides. The vast majority of resorts around the world are now snowboard-friendly, with accredited snowboarding schools and professionally trained instructors, terrain parks, halfpipes and equipment for hire. This mainstream acceptance means one thing for you: there has never been a better time to take up snowboarding, and the amenities abound, making it easy, safe and fun.

The sport is no longer the sole domain of the

above A BACKCOUNTRY RIDER ADJUSTS HER AVALANCHE TRANSCEIVER, A RADIO SIGNALLING DEVICE USED TO LOCATE BURIED AVALANCHE VICTIMS. BACKCOUNTRY RIDING IS AN EXCITING DISCIPLINE TO TRY ONCE YOU HAVE MASTERED THE BASICS.

opposite POPULAR DEMAND AT SNOW RESORTS WORLDWIDE, LIKE SAAS FEE IN SWITZERLAND, HAS OPENED MOST TERRAIN TO BOARDERS AND TURNED SNOWBOARDING INTO A MAINSTREAM SPORT.

HIKING UPHILL FOR ANOTHER RUN IN THE HALFPIPE PROVIDES AN EXCELLENT PHYSICAL WORKOUT.

manic teenage set. Young people do make up a significant portion of the snowboarding community, but as the sport continues to mature so does its demographic base, and newcomers of all ages are getting hooked. Also, it's no longer just for men – about a third of all enthusiasts are women. This factor has led to the development of more top-quality snowboarding equipment and clothing designed to accommodate their specific requirements. Children-specific equipment, clothing and protective gear has developed as well.

One of the main reasons for snowboarding's explosion in popularity is that it is relatively easy to learn the basics. It only takes about three days to learn the skills you need to ride. Through a gradual series of lessons and exercises that reinforce basic movements while building confidence, most beginners starting from scratch or making the transition from skiing do so with ease — some people get the hang of it in as little as a day.

Another plus is that once you've mastered the basics, it's easy to improve. After learning to ride with control and confidence, a whole spectrum of disciplines awaits you, from freestyle riding to carving and all-mountain freeriding. Naturally, it will take time before you are launching airs in the terrain park, but getting there is half of the fun — and seeing a marked improvement in your abilities every day you ride is half of the thrill.

It's good for you too!

It might be hard to believe that something so fun could actually be good for you, but the workout you get from a day of snowboarding is the perfect mix of aerobic and anaerobic activity. Since snowboarding concentrates heavily on lower body movement, you will need to rely on your quadriceps, hamstrings, gluteal and hip and calf muscles. The movements made as you crank out toeside and heelside turns down the mountain will steadily increase your strength in these muscle groups.

Riding incorporates plenty of upper body activity, too; your abdominal muscles, lower back and obliques (the muscles along the sides of your torso) will develop. Additionally, you are guaranteed to increase your overall flexibility. You may also find that the muscle workout you get from riding is superior to any exercise regime you have encountered. Most fitness experts believe that at least 20 to 30 minutes of aerobic activity a day is needed to stay in shape or improve your overall condition — this is about the length of an average run. The best part: you will be having too much fun to notice that you are doing your body a favour.

More good news

Whether you are a crossover skier or someone who has never set foot on snow before, the chapters that follow will provide you with everything you need to know in order to embark on your journey toward snowboarding bliss. You'll get the lowdown on snow-boarding equipment: how it works, how to choose the right gear for your needs, and what to wear for warmth, comfort and safety. A step-by-step approach to learning and practicing the basic fundamental skills needed to snowboard will help you progress, safely and speedily, to your first turns. A comprehensive overview of the range of disciplines that the sport offers will assist you in progressing beyond the basics as soon as you feel confident enough.

If you're not familiar with the slopes or with alpine environments in general, you may benefit from a few words on safety and the 'rules of the road'. To end with there's a list of recommended snowboarding organisations and resorts around the world, which will ensure that you know where to go when you are ready to plan your own endless winter.

LEARNING TO RIDE IS EASY AND FUN — MAKING SNOWBOARDING A PERFECT CHOICE FOR PEOPLE OF ALL AGES.

Boards, Boots and Bindings

getting the right snowboarding equipment used to be a cinch, as just a handful of companies made a small range of basic items. Nowadays it's become slightly more complicated; there's been an explosion of brands entering the market and the specialization of the sport has created many choices for each riding style and every rider's preference. While this is great for riders, the increased variety has complicated the matter. Understanding the key elements of the equipment will make your first snowboarding experience easier and guide you when buying a setup of your own.

What kind of rider are you?

Before you get started — and long before you consider buying your own equipment — you need to answer this: what kind of riding are you planning to do?

Do you want to boost 'big airs' (perform jumps) in the terrain park and ride the halfpipe or could you not care less if your board never left the ground? Do you dream of solitude and knee-deep powder snow, or do you want to lay down top-speed turns on trackless groomed runs (known as 'corduroy')? Whatever your personal passion, choosing the right board setup for your style of riding is the secret of your future success. If you are not entirely convinced that one or other discipline is for you, bear in mind that your choice doesn't have to be a permanent one. Many snowboarding enthusiasts are tempted to dabble in more than one discipline until they find the one they enjoy the most. Boards come in three main categories: freestyle, freeride and alpine carving/race boards.

opposite FREESTYLE BOARDS HAVE MINIMAL SWING WEIGHT AND SOFT BOOTS OFFER MAXIMUM FLEXIBILITY — IMPORTANT FEATURES FOR RIDERS WHO PERFORM TRICKS IN THE HALFPIPE.

Features of freestyle boards

■ These boards are made for trick riding, if you're planning to spend most of your time in the halfpipe or the terrain park, this is the setup for you.

■ Freestyle boards tend to be short (for less swing weight when performing spinning tricks) and for manoeuvrability in the halfpipe.

■ A softer flex pattern (see p 14) and greater overall width make these boards a little slower.

■ This means they are an ideal choice for those just starting out in the sport.

■ Most are of twin-tip construction, i.e. the nose and tail ends are identical in shape. The board can thus be ridden 'fakie' (tail-end first).

■ Freestyle setups normally feature soft boots with plenty of flex and bindings that offer moderate to low support around the ankles.

Features of freeride boards

■ These boards are an excellent choice if you want to be an all-mountain rider and be able to handle all types of terrain.

■ Freeride boards tend to be stiffer than freestyle boards but are still suitable for a variety of terrain types and conditions.

■ Freeride boards are longer and narrower than freestyle boards, allowing for more precise turning.

■ Many also feature a directional flex pattern with a distinct nose and tail-end, making them an excellent choice for beginners.

■ This means they're best ridden forward, but may be ridden fakie as well.

■ Freeride setups normally feature soft boots and bindings that provide more support than freestyle boots and bindings.

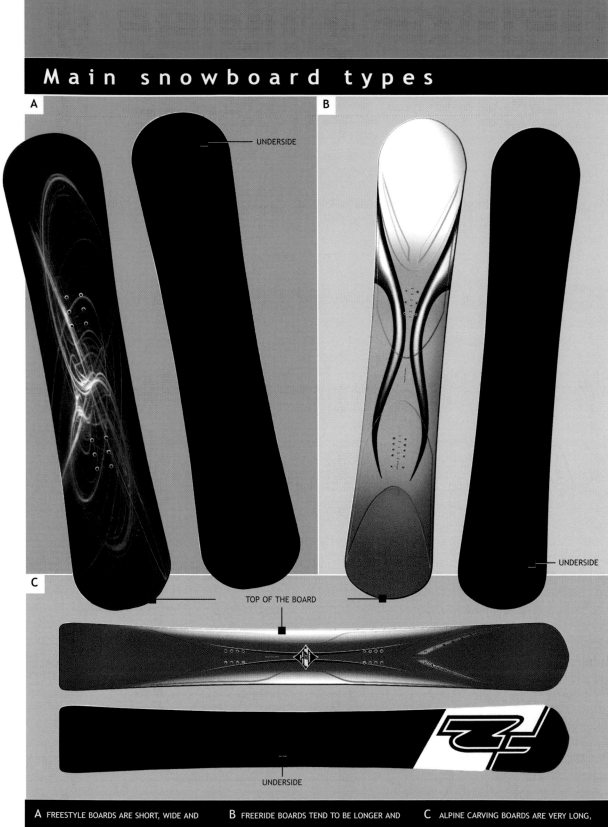

A   UNDERSIDE

B   UNDERSIDE

TOP OF THE BOARD

C   UNDERSIDE

A FREESTYLE BOARDS ARE SHORT, WIDE AND FLEXIBLE, MAKING THEM GREAT FOR SPINNING TRICKS, AERIAL AND RIDING FAKIE.

B FREERIDE BOARDS TEND TO BE LONGER AND NARROWER, ALLOWING FOR MORE VERSATILITY.

C ALPINE CARVING BOARDS ARE VERY LONG, NARROW AND RIGID FOR HIGH-SPEED RIDING AND ENHANCED EDGE-TO-EDGE ABILITY.

Features of alpine carving/race boards:

■ Their narrow waist width makes for a super-tight turning radius and lightning-fast edge-to-edge ability.

■ Their stiff construction keeps the board stable at high speeds, but their general lack of 'give' does not make them ideal for the first-time snowboard rider.

■ This type of board has little or no tail kick, which means it is not designed to ride fakie.

■ Alpine carving and race boards are always paired with hard boots (similar to traditional ski boots) and plate bindings. As with ski bindings, these consist of plastic or metal plates firmly attached to the board.

Key factors to bear in mind when buying your board

WAIST WIDTH: The board's width at its narrowest point is the first important factor to consider.

■ Size counts: a board that's too narrow for the size of your feet will allow them to hang over the board's edges.

■ Conversely, a board that is too wide for your foot size will result in a loss of responsiveness and, therefore, decrease your level of control.

■ This is a handy rule of thumb: if your shoe size is 10.5 (European size 45) or larger, you need a board with a minimum waist width of 26cm (10in).

■ If your shoe size is 8 (European size 41) or smaller, look for a board with a waist width of 25cm (9.5in) or less.

LENGTH: The ideal board should be about 90 per cent of your own height. If you stand the board up in front of you, its 'nose' should come up to about the level of your chin.

■ Personal preference as to your potential snowboarding activities will dictate the best board length for you.

■ If you're planning to do plenty of powder and all-mountain riding, go for more length.

■ If you'd prefer to do most of your snowboarding in the park and half-pipe, choose a shorter board.

■ For the male rider of average height, the best choice is a board about 160—70cm (5ft 3in—5ft 6in) in length.

■ For the average female snowboarder, the correct length would be around 150—60cm (5ft—5ft 3in).

FLEX PATTERN: Again, personal preference plays a role. The amount of flexibility you choose relates to both your body weight and your riding style.

■ A more rigid flex pattern offers a greater responsiveness when turning — an ideal choice for carving.

■ A softer flex will lessen the board's responsiveness, but is the better choice for freestyle riding.

■ Keep in mind that this is relative; firm flex for a 68kg (150lb) rider will seem soft to a 90kg (200lb) rider.

■ Don't forget the board's torsional flex; softer torsion will make it much easier to get in and out of a turn, while a torsionally stiffer board will be able to hold the edge more effectively in the turn.

SHAPE: Most boards take one of three shape patterns: directional, directional twin and twin tip.

■ Most all-mountain riders opt for a directional shape (meaning that while the board can be ridden regular or fakie, it works best when ridden forward).

■ 'Twin tip' boards are symmetrical lengthwise, so that the board can be ridden either forward or fakie with ease, making this the best choice for freestyle.

■ Directional twins are a hybrid of these two; the twin-tip shape incorporates a directional flex pattern, which means the best of all worlds.

PRICE: If you want to buy the latest model, expect to pay a high price. But you don't always have to spend a lot.

■ To save on equipment, buy during the off-season as prices are always higher at the start of a new season.

■ At the end of the season shops are eager to offload their current stock and will often have plenty of equipment on offer at bargain prices.

■ A good idea is to check local shops for used equipment.

■ Riders who can afford it are keen to acquire each season's next fashionable board and are often happy to part with their 'old' equipment quite cheaply.

REGARDLESS OF YOUR preferred style of riding, your snowboard is the most important tool of your new trade, so it helps to have a good understanding of its construction.

The TIP of the snowboard (also known as the nose) is the forward end.

■ The tip curves upward, to allow the board to ride on top of the snow.

■ Freestyle and freeride boards have more 'kick' in the nose than does an alpine carving board, because freeride boards are designed for use in a variety of different conditions and types of terrain.

The board's TAIL is, not surprisingly, the rear end. It has an upturned edge to help the board release from a turn.

■ As with the tip, the 'kick' in the tail is more pronounced in freestyle and freeride models.

The BASE of the board is the underside that makes contact with the snow.

■ The base is made of a hard polyethylene base that holds wax well and allows for maximum glide. This material is hardy, but can be gouged if ridden over rocks and other debris.

■ Bases may be either sintered or extruded. (These terms refer to the polyethylene or P-tex used to construct a board.)

■ Boards with sintered bases tend to be more expensive than those with extruded bases, but they are more resistant to damage and tend to absorb and hold wax better than boards with extruded bases. On the other hand, extruded bases cost less and are easy to repair.

The CORE of the board is either made of durable foam or wood, which is then enclosed in a fibreglass shell.

■ The core section is the element responsible for giving the board its flex and spring.

The DECK is the top of the board, on which the bindings are mounted.

■ The deck is covered with a TOPSHEET that protects the core of the board.

The BINDING INSERTS are recessed, threaded steel holes that take the screws which hold the bindings to the deck.

■ The inserts are arranged in a pattern so a rider is able to adjust the bindings to his or her own stance width and angle (for more on this see p 23).

The STOMP PAD is a small rubber pad attached to the deck of the board between the front and rear bindings. This is used for traction when the rider skates over flat areas and whenever the rider's rear foot is not strapped into the bindings. It is especially useful for beginners.

SIDEWALLS are the protective elements that cover the core between the deck and the base.

■ Sidewalls are only used in boards of the 'sandwich' style of construction.

■ In the case of boards made with 'cap' construction, the sidewalls are left out. This means that the board's topsheet extends over the sides to the edges of the board.

EDGES are the steel strips that run along either side of the board's base.

■ The sharp edges cut into the snow, allowing control of the board in turning and stopping.

The BINDINGS are not technically part of the board, but they provide the vital interface between rider and board.

■ Bindings come in one of two different types: soft-boot setup and hard-boot setup. (See pp 20-25 for more information).

The LEASH is a cord attached to the front binding that fastens around the ankle of the rider's forward leg.

- The safety leash is designed to keep the board from sliding away when your feet are not locked into the bindings.

- Leashes are usually mandatory, as a speeding board without a rider can be dangerous to others.

- Most resorts and ski areas do not allow snowboard riders to use the lifts if they do not have a safety leash.

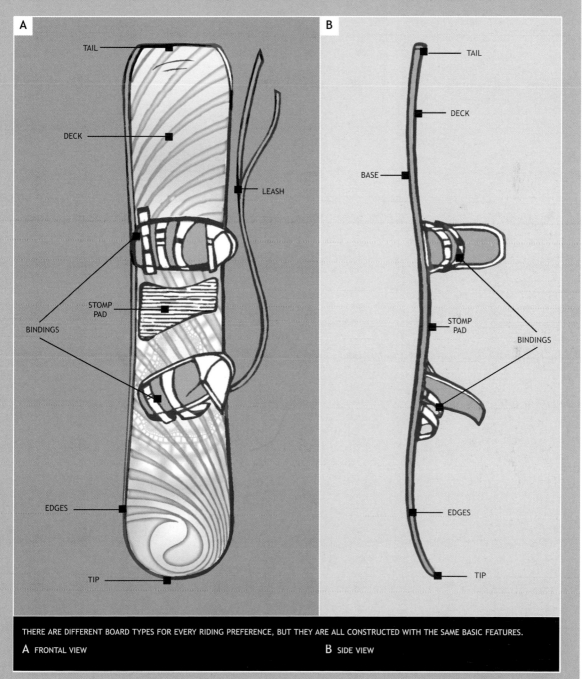

THERE ARE DIFFERENT BOARD TYPES FOR EVERY RIDING PREFERENCE, BUT THEY ARE ALL CONSTRUCTED WITH THE SAME BASIC FEATURES.

A FRONTAL VIEW

B SIDE VIEW

Boot types

A STANDARD FREESTYLE BOOT LINER.

B THE FLEXIBILITY OF THIS SOFT FREESTYLE BOOT MAKES IT IDEAL FOR MANOEUVRES.

C A FREERIDE BOOT HAS UPPER-BOOT SUPPORT FOR ADDED RESPONSIVENESS.

D ALPINE CARVING BOOTS ARE SIMILIAR TO SKI BOOTS, WITH MAXIMUM SUPPORT.

E BOOTS FOR WOMEN ACCOMMODATE FEMALE FOOT SIZE AND SHAPE TO PREVENT HEEL LIFT WHILE RIDING.

F BOOTS FOR KIDS ARE DESIGNED FOR CHILD-SIZED FEET AND ABILITY LEVELS.

G THIS STEP-IN BOOT IS FAIRLY RIGID WITH ITS BUILT-IN HEELSIDE SUPPORT AND ANKLE STRAP.

The shape of the board

A board's FLEX PATTERN controls the extent to which the board bends, and where. If you hold a board upright and push on the centre of the deck, you can easily see how the flex pattern allows it to bend throughout the middle.

■ CAMBER is the board's built-in 'spring'. Lay the board down, deck uppermost, on the floor. You'll see that it doesn't lie flat, but arches upward in the middle, which allows for ease of turning. When you initiate a turn, you set the 'spring' which will promptly begin to snap back to its original position and help to push you through the turn.

■ TORSION refers to the amount of lateral flex in the board. To understand this, imagine standing the board on its end, and trying to twist the board as if its centre were a waist. A board with more torsional flex offers a more forgiving ride; greater rigidity means added responsiveness during turns.

■ SIDECUT is the amount of width difference between the board's tip, tail and 'waist'. Snowboards are narrower in the centre than at the ends. This hourglass shape assists the board's turning ability — the deeper the sidecut, the tighter the turns a rider is able to make.

Tips on buying a board

Don't be surprised if you feel confused by the wide variety of sizes and shapes when you start looking around to buy a board. An expensive mistake is to see the latest model in the store window featuring cool graphics and a pro rider's signature on the glossy deck — and slap down the credit card.

Now you're out of the shop, clutching your new acquisition, ready to try out the board. Halfway through your first turn, your toes drag in the snow. You're dismayed to discover that your new board is too narrow for you, and it's back to square one.

Snowboards aren't cheap, so it's important to consider your choice. That way, you will ensure that you have the right board for your preferred type of riding and that it will perform well.

Boots

Freestyle and freeride snowboarding boots are known as SOFT BOOTS. They are similar in appearance to regular lace-up snow boots, and constructed of leather and canvas with rubber soles. They are as warm and comfortable as regular snow boots.

Hard boots are worn by alpine carving and race enthusiasts, and crossover skiers will find them comfortable as they resemble traditional ski boots. However, they do have major functional differences.

Features of soft boots:

■ The soles are short and bevelled at the heel and toe to minimize foot drag (the amount of the boot that projects beyond the edges of the board).

■ The upper portion of the boot has a built-in support for ease in transferring the movement of the leg to the board, and built-in forward lean which makes it easier to achieve the bent-knee stance.

■ Soft-boot manufacturers make a wide range of different models which are suitable for freeride and freestyle riders. The main difference in these models is in the degree of boot flex; more flex for freestyle riding, firmer support for freeriding.

■ Freeride models feature a stiffer upper boot and a higher cuff with a lace-up inner boot which enhances its firmness.

■ Freestyle models usually have loose, moulded-foam inner boots to maximize their flexibility.

Features of hard boots:

■ A hard boot comprises a moulded plastic outer shell, which fastens with strong metal clips, and a stitched, padded inner boot. The benefit of the plastic shell is that it gives riders more power and precision in edging movements.

■ Hard boots also feature built-in forward lean and a high upper-boot that reaches the top of the calf, for added support.

■ Hard boots have a stiff but responsive fit that provides maximum control at high speeds. However, they are not suitable for freestyle acrobatic manoeuvres as they limit the amount of flexibility.

Bindings: The all-important ties that bind

Bindings are the vital interface between you and your board. Their primary function is to transfer the movements of your body to the board you ride on, in the most efficient manner.

There are three specific types of bindings to choose from — soft-boot bindings, hard-boot bindings and soft-boot step-ins.

Soft-boot bindings

All soft boot bindings are similar in construction. The baseplate, made of metal or plastic or a combination of the two, is fastened to the deck of the board. It holds your foot securely in place by means of two or three adjustable, cushioned straps.

Unlike traditional ski bindings, soft-boot bindings used by snowboarders do not have a quick-release system, so if you fall, you stay strapped in.

The highback is a vertical support made of moulded plastic or carbon-fibre that is attached to the baseplate of the binding. The boot's back rests on the highback, which offers support (and leverage) during a heelside turn.

■ FREESTYLE BINDINGS are the most popular choice. They are comfortable and versatile, providing the rider with a feeling of freedom. Freestyle and all-mountain riders prefer this type of binding. They are as appropriate for riding in the halfpipe as they are for making powder runs.

Freestyle bindings feature a lower-cut highback for maximum flexibility, and hold the feet firmly in place with two sturdy straps. One comes just above the toe of the boot, and the other at the ankle. While freestyle bindings are a good general choice, it is worth bearing in mind that what you will gain in flexibility, you will lose in responsiveness.

What to look for when buying boots

Having the right pair of boots is crucial; your choice of boot may make the difference to your pleasure in snowboarding, between hours of excruciating pain or days of blissful comfort. That's why you should always keep comfort and fit in mind when choosing boots.

As with any athletic footwear, FIT is the most important factor to ensure comfort and performance.

■ Snowboarding boots should fit snugly around the ankle, and should hold your heel firmly down in the boot.

■ Heel lift should be eliminated completely when the boot is laced up. (If you can lift your heel at all, the boots don't fit properly.) Many models of boots are designed with this in mind, and have built-in heel 'cups' to minimize lift.

■ Overall fit is much the same as with any other boot, bearing in mind that the boot's internal padding will become compacted, increasing the available space slightly once they've been ridden in a few times.

■ Some brands tend to be a better fit for broader or narrower feet. The shop assistants should be able to advise you on this aspect. Boots are also designed specifically for the needs of women and children.

FLEX plays a role in guiding your choice of boots. Consider your riding style and preference when deciding how much flex you require.

■ Freeride boots usually feature stiffer upper boots for added support, as well as lace-up liners that allow you to adjust the amount of flexibility.

■ Freestyle models tend to be lower cut with loose moulded inner liners.

PRICE is a key point. Good, solid boots are quite expensive, and the cheapest boots are not always the best buy. You don't need to buy the most fashionable, top-of-the-range boots, but a good pair that fit really well and are designed for your riding style will be an excellent investment. They will also enhance the pleasure of your snowboarding experience.

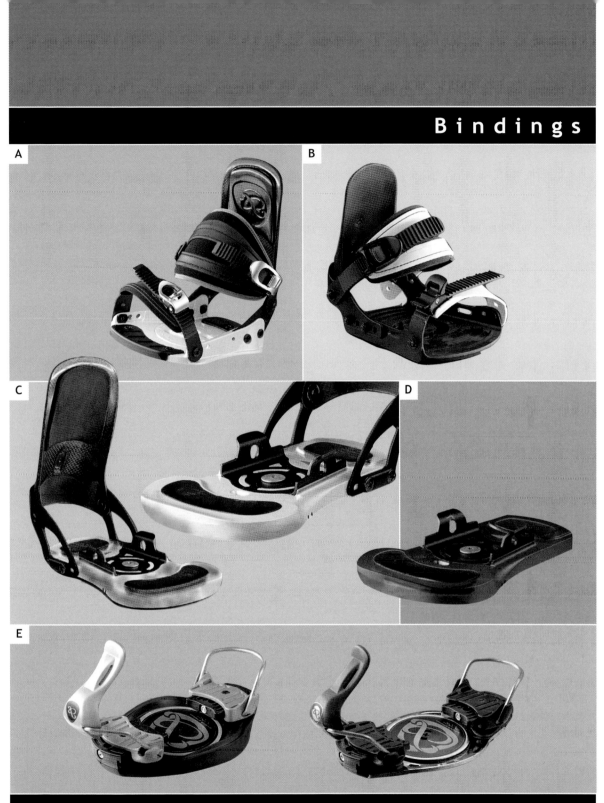

A THESE SOFT FREERIDE BINDINGS HAVE TWO ALUMINIUM BUCKLES WHICH CAN BE OPENED QUICKLY, WHILE THE TALLER HIGHBACKS PROVIDE A DIRECT TRANSFER OF CONTROL AND POWER.

B FREESTYLE BINDINGS HAVE TWO SUPPORT STRAPS AND LOW HIGHBACKS TO MAXIMIZE FLEXIBILITY.

C SOME STEP-IN BINDINGS STILL INCORPORATE HIGHBACKS, BUT INSTEAD OF STRAPS, INCLUDE A SPECIAL INTERLOCKING MECHANISM THAT ATTACHES THE BOOT FIRMLY TO THE BASE.

D OTHER STEP-IN DESIGNS HAVE NO HIGHBACKS AND INSTEAD HEELSIDE SUPPORT IS BUILT INTO THE BOOT ITSELF.

E PLATE BINDINGS ARE ULTRA-RESPONSIVE AND COMPATIBLE ONLY WITH HARD BOOTS, SIMILAR TO THOSE USED FOR SKIING.

What to look for when buying bindings:

The manufacturers of riding equipment all do their best to enhance comfort and performance while keeping bindings light and durable. However, the number of new models on the market continues to grow. This is a benefit as you're bound to find bindings to suit you, but it's worth your while to do some homework before you buy.

■ FIT — in relation to your boots — is a key factor. Take the boots with you when you shop and make absolutely sure that they fit snugly into the bindings' baseplates. Also, check the height of the highback. Higher highbacks offer increased responsiveness, while lower ones mean greater flexibility. Make sure the highback height matches the height of your boots. A highback that is lower than the boot will result in loss of leverage. By contrast, a highback that is higher than the boot will press against your calf, which may become painful.

■ COMFORT and ADJUSTABILITY are also important. Check out where the straps grip your boots and ratchet them down to make sure they don't squeeze your feet. Ensure that the baseplate features plenty of screw-hole combinations, so you can fine-tune your stance angle. Also make sure that the highbacks and straps are fully adjustable to customize fit, forward lean and highback angle. Bindings should feel comfortable immediately when you strap into them but remember that it's always good to havea range of adjustment options, in case you need them later on.

■ PRICE may have a bearing on the decision you make with regard to your choice of bindings. Try not to skimp on your selection as bindings are vital to your safety and the enjoyment of riding your board. Prices vary according to the materials employed in their manufacture. All-plastic bindings are generally cheaper, and plastic baseplates can provide some flex and cushioning, but may not be sufficiently durable.

Metal-and-plastic combinations retain flexibility, while reinforcing stability in the heel cup. However, more metal equals more weight. Carbon-based bindings combine durability and responsiveness with lightness, but they are more expensive as their manufacturing costs are higher.

■ FREERIDE BINDINGS are similar to freestyle bindings, although they have a taller, more supportive highback, and a third strap that fastens around the shin. The added height of back support and the extra strap provide greater leverage for enhanced board control while still maintaining a soft-boot setup. If you don't necessarily need the flexibility of freestyle bindings, these are a good choice.

Hard boot or plate bindings

These bindings are typically used with hard boots and alpine carving/race boards, and are as close to a traditional ski binding as a snowboard interface can get. Plate bindings consist of a small metal base plate and two flexible wire metal bails that hook onto the heel and the toe of the boot. Their rigid responsiveness provides maximum leverage and power for high-speed carving and riding on hard snow.

Soft-boot step-ins

These bindings make for a soft-boot interface without straps. They are easy to get in and out of, while still maintaining the soft-boot feel.

The first step-ins began appearing in 1994 with K2's Clicker setup. Today, many firms have entered the step-in market and each have their own designs, so there is nothing standard about step-in bindings.

Traditionalists baulk at the control that is lost with a no-strap interface, and many soft-boot riders choose to stick with the trusty strap method. Manufacturers continue to develop innovative strap bindings in an effort to increase comfort.

The bottom line is that the choice of whether to step in or strap in depends on personal preference. If you feel that the convenience of stepping in outweighs the attendant loss of control, then it is best to go for that particular style of binding.

Mounting and adjusting your bindings

Mounting your bindings to the board is more complicated than merely lining up the holes on each binding's base plate with the board's inserts.

Once you've established whether you are goofy or regular (these terms used for variations in stance are explained on pp 38-39) you need to fine-tune your setup to a stance that works for you and your riding style. Most boards have several sets of inserts for adjusting stance width and location, and almost all bindings have rotating discs in their baseplates for adjusting stance angle.

You will need a Philips screwdriver and an Allen wrench or two, and it would be worth your while to acquire some basic knowledge of stance width, stance location and stance angle.

STANCE WIDTH refers to the distance between your front and your rear foot.
■ A basic stance width is about 30 per cent of your height. (Check that your feet are roughly your shoulders' width apart.)
■ For freestyle riders, this needs to be a little wider, about 48-61cm (19-24in) apart.
■ The extra width will reduce the board's swing weight and make it easier to perform different jumping and spinning tricks.
■ If you opt for a hard-boot setup, this should be somewhat narrower, about 38-46cm (15-18in) apart; to maximize the shape and flex of the board for carving turns.
■ A good freeride stance reference point would fall between the two, 43-51cm (17-20in) apart.

STANCE LOCATION refers to the location of the centre point between your bindings in relation to the centre of the snowboard. Since freestyle boards tend to be twin-tips, the common freestyle stance is in the centre, with each binding positioned the same distance away from the corresponding tip.
■ This centre stance allows the rider to take full advantage of the snowboard's ability to be ridden either forward or fakie.

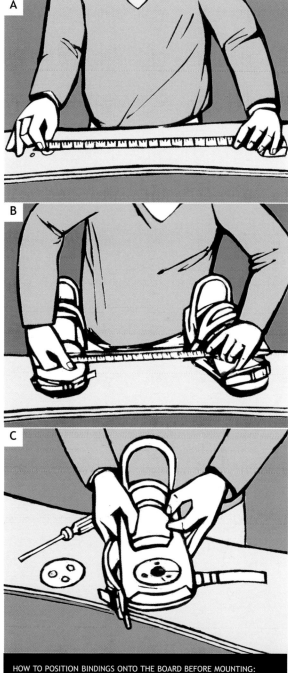

HOW TO POSITION BINDINGS ONTO THE BOARD BEFORE MOUNTING:
A STANCE WIDTH SHOULD BE SHOULDERS' WIDTH APART.
B STANCE LOCATION SHOULD START OUT CENTRED, OR SLIGHTLY IN THE 'BACK SEAT'.
C STANCE ANGLE SHOULD BE LOWER (STRAIGHTER ACROSS THE BOARD'S LENGTH) FOR A FREESTYLE STANCE AND HIGHER (TOWARDS THE BOARD'S NOSE) FOR A NARROWER CARVING STANCE.

■ Most freeriders and carvers prefer a stance location of 2.5-5cm (1-2in) behind the centre.

■ Locating the bindings 'in the back seat' like this (known as a directional stance), works well with a directional board's flex pattern, and it helps to keep the board's nose up when riding powder.

STANCE ANGLE refers to the angle of the bindings across the board's longitudinal axis, in which zero degrees represents a line perpendicular to the board's length (see diagram below).

■ Your back binding should generally be mounted at a less acute angle than the front one.

■ Freestyle riders should start with a stance angle somewhere between 0–15 degrees (A).

■ Freeriders usually start with a 30-degree angle in front and about a 15-degree angle at the back (B).

■ Alpine riders accommodate narrow board widths and fast edge-to-edge movements, so aim for 55 degrees in front and 50 degrees at the back (C).

■ Novice carvers should reduce this by about 10 degrees on each binding.

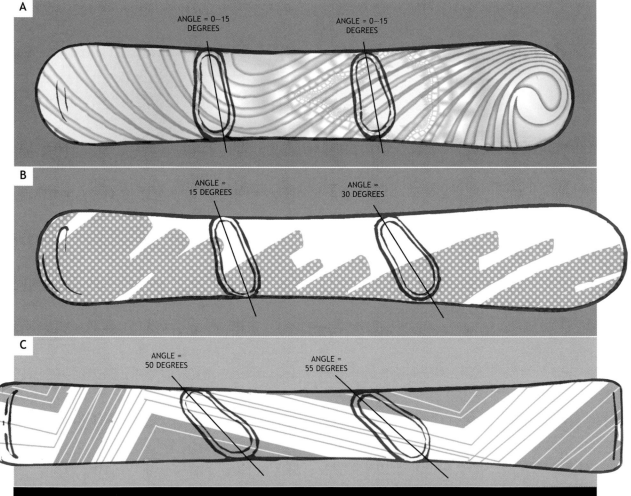

A

ANGLE = 0–15 DEGREES

ANGLE = 0–15 DEGREES

B

ANGLE = 15 DEGREES

ANGLE = 30 DEGREES

C

ANGLE = 50 DEGREES

ANGLE = 55 DEGREES

VARIATIONS IN STANCE ANGLE

A A WIDER STANCE WITH A LOW STANCE ANGLE IS BEST FOR FREESTYLE TRICKS AND RIDING FAKIE.

B FREERIDERS OFTEN CHOOSE SLIGHTLY HIGHER ANGLES, WITH THE BINDINGS BACK FOR POWDER RIDING.

C A VERY NARROW STANCE WITH A HIGH STANCE ANGLE ALLOWS FOR THE LIGHTNING-FAST EDGE CHANGING THAT CARVING REQUIRES.

Adjusting the bindings

Once the bindings are mounted, you'll need to fine-tune your setup to maximize its comfort and performance. Most bindings have built-in adjustment capacity so that customizing your stance setup is usually quite a simple task.

Start with the board's FORWARD LEAN (the amount of forward angle on the highback support).

■ Adding more forward lean will give you more leverage and make your heelside turning more responsive. This will also force the knees to bend, to ensure a good riding stance.

■ Don't overdo it; too much forward lean creates too much knee bend. This, in turn, will put pressure on your quadricep muscles and reduce your ability to turn easily.

■ In most soft-boot bindings, adjusting the forward lean is usually just a matter of changing the position of a plastic stay behind the highback.

ROTATING THE HIGHBACKS is also a simple matter, if the bindings allow for it. If so, there will be slots on the hinges where the highbacks are attached to the binding's baseplate.

■ Loosen the bolts and rotate the highbacks so that they're parallel with the board's heelside edge.

■ This will make heelside turning more responsive than would be the case if the highbacks remained angled along with the baseplate.

ADJUSTING STRAP POSITION usually involves unscrewing the straps from the baseplate and moving them forward or back on the bindings (if the bindings allow for this, there will be extra holes on the baseplate).

■ Moving the straps higher up on the foot improves control. On the other hand, if you move them so that they rest lower down, it will increase flexibility.

■ The toe strap should rest around the base of the toes and hold the tip of the boot firmly down.

■ It's also possible to alter the length of the strap to conform to your foot size. If you find yourself pulling on the straps just to get a snug fit, shorten them by

attaching them to the baseplate further along the length of the strap. Most straps have extra holes to provide for this adjustment.

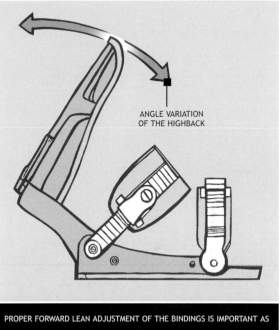

ANGLE VARIATION OF THE HIGHBACK

PROPER FORWARD LEAN ADJUSTMENT OF THE BINDINGS IS IMPORTANT AS IT DIRECTLY AFFECTS THE AMOUNT OF KNEE BEND IN YOUR STANCE.

Waxing and tuning: Board maintenance

Think of your snowboard as a form of transport; just as with your car or your bicycle, it will need some maintenance to keep it running smoothly.

It's just a matter of time. Eventually wax wears off, edges become dull and sooner or later you're bound to run over a branch or a rock that takes a gouge out of your board's base. You could just take it in to the shop for a wax and tune every so often, but learning how to do it yourself will save you time and money.

For a small initial outlay you can get all the tools you need for basic maintenance. You probably already have some of the necessary items at home. Several complex repair jobs call for a professional repairman with specialized equipment, but for simple day-to-day maintenance, follow the advice overleaf and you'll be able to give your board a tuneup that's every bit as good as that offered by a shop.

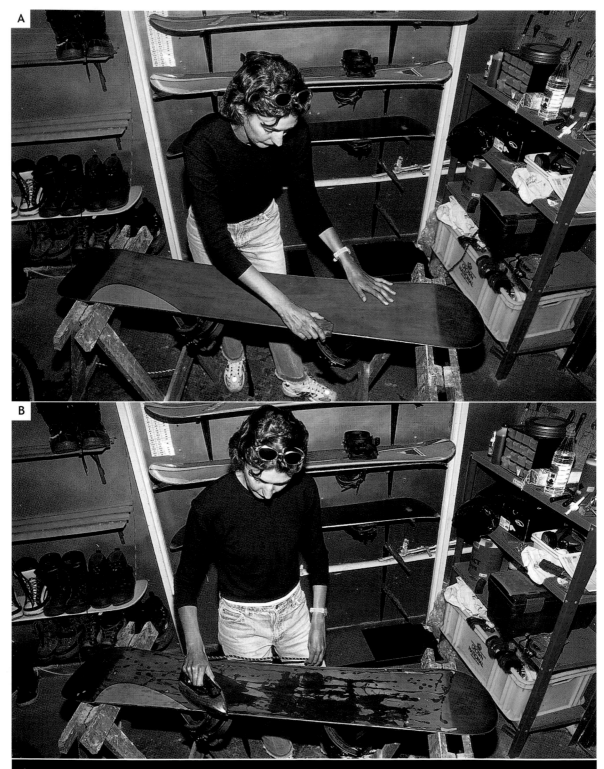

A SHARPENING AND DETUNING YOUR EDGES WILL ENHANCE YOUR BOARD'S OVERALL PERFORMANCE.

B WAXING YOUR BOARD PROTECTS YOUR BOARD'S BASE AND ALLOWS FOR MAXIMUM GLIDE.

Sharpening the edges

First, find an area that you can work in without worrying about making a mess; a garage would be perfect. Cover the floor with newspaper, to catch shavings.

You'll need: a file and file guide, a rag or towel, and a gummy stone or detuning device (a device to remove some of the 'bite' from the edges after they have been sharpened). Although a mounted vice is ideal for holding the board, you can just as easily hold it edge-up between your knees.

■ First, wipe the edges down with a rag. Then run a deburring stone along the edges to smooth them down and take off any scraps of metal that may have been gouged from the base. Now you are ready to begin sharpening the edges.

■ Remember that there are two sides to each of the board's edges: the base edge and the sidewall edge. Start with the sidewall edge.

■ When you begin filing, make sure that the file stays perfectly flat and even along the edge — the file guide is important here.

■ Using the file guide to hold the file at a perfect right angle, gently run it lengthwise along the edge until the edge feels smooth. Remove excess shavings from the file from time to time.

■ A few passes should do the trick; remember you have a limited amount of edge metal on your board, so it's better not to remove too much.

■ Once you're satisfied with the feel of the sidewall edge, repeat the process on the base edge, then do the other side of the board.

Detuning

You may want to DETUNE the board's edges once they are sharpened to enhance your riding performance.

■ Essentially, detuning rounds off the right angle created on the board's edge by sharpening and keeps the edge from digging into the snow.

■ By taking some of the bite out of the board's edges it will reduce the chance of your board catching an edge, which may make you fall over.

■ Most file guides allow for adjustment of the guide angle to detune the edge.

■ Set the file guide to about one degree and carefully run the file lengthwise along the board.

■ Again, remember you can always take more edge off later if necessary, but once you've shaved the metal, it's lost for good.

Waxing

Waxing your board is essential; it protects the base and allows for maximum glide when you're riding. You should wax the board whenever the underside feels dry, or when conditions change (there are several different types of wax for different snow temperatures and conditions).

Once you realize how easy it is to wax your board, you'll wonder why you ever considered paying someone else to do it.

To get started, you'll need: a rag or towel, snowboard wax, an iron (one that you no longer need; once you apply wax to it, you won't want to use it on clothes again) and a plastic scraper. As with edge sharpening, this is a messy job, so be prepared.

■ Heat the iron to medium temperature. Place the board base-up on the floor and wipe it down with a rag or towel to remove any dirt.

■ Once the iron is warm, hold it above the base, nose down, and press the wax against the metal.

DIFFERENT WAXES ARE AVAILABLE FOR EVERY SNOW TEMPERATURE. MANY RIDERS CHOOSE A GENERAL-PURPOSE WAX THAT WORKS WELL IN MOST CONDITIONS.

■ When the wax starts dripping, move the iron back and forth over the base to allow the droplets to cover the majority of its surface.

■ Now run the iron over the base again and smooth the wax out until it covers the entire area.

■ As with ironing a shirt, be careful not to leave the iron sitting in one place too long.

■ Once the base is coated, let the wax cool for an hour or two (overnight if possible), allowing it to be absorbed into the fibres of the base.

■ Then use the plastic scraper to drag across the board's base and scrape off the excess wax.

■ Sweep up the shavings, clean up the mess and you're ready to ride.

Fixing base gouges

It's inevitable — however careful you are, at some point you will take a gouge out of the base of your board. Gouges can range from minor scratches to deep ruts that affect the edges and reach right into the board's inner core. You may be able to repair this type of damage at home, but you might be better off taking your board into the shop where a skilled expert has the right tools to fix it properly.

■ Adding p-tex (polyethylene) to the board's base entails melting a p-tex candle and filling the gouge, then scraping and sanding the area down to make the damaged area flush with the rest of the board. However, melting a p-tex candle by lighting it makes it difficult to drip the melting compound without getting black carbon residue on the board. This will fill the gouge, but may cause cosmetic damage. Fumes from molten plastic can also be dangerous when inhaled and an accidental drip on the skin could cause a painful wound.

■ Most shops have special tools to melt p-tex without burning it. Also, a well-equipped shop is likely to have a computerized base grinder to restore the base perfectly once the gouges are filled. Fixing gouges is a specialized job best left to the professionals.

TO PREPARE YOUR BOARD FOR OFF-SEASON STORAGE, WIPE THE BASE WITH A CLEAN RAG AND SOLVENT TO REMOVE ANY GRIME BUILDUP, THEN GIVE IT A GOOD COAT OF WARM-WEATHER WAX.

IN MOST PARTS OF THE WORLD, snowboarding is a seasonal sport. For a large part of the year your board will be collecting dust until next year's snow falls, while you wait for the long off-season to finally drag to an end.

A few snowboarders might be tempted to strap on the board and flop around in the living room a few times during the summer, but most people plan to store it safely until next year.

Tips on preparing your board for storage

■ First, wipe the board down with a citrus solvent to remove dirt and road grime.

■ Apply a coat of warm-weather (yellow) wax to the base of the snowboard to protect it. You can even leave the excess wax on the base and wait till next season to scrape and polish it off.

■ Finally, use an oil-based lubricant like WD-40 or synthetic bike chain lubricant and wipe a very thin layer onto the board's edges with a clean rag to keep them from rusting. Be careful not to get oil onto the sidewalls and base of the board.

■ Put your board in a board bag or wrap it in a clean sheet and store it in a cool, dry place. If possible, store the base of your board up in an overhead rack.

■ Make sure your boots are completely dry before putting them away, especially if they are leather and you plan to stow them in a canvas board bag. It's also wise to give your bindings a quick wipe-down and fasten the straps.

■ When the season rolls around, scrape the wax off, wipe down your rust-free edges, use a gummy stone to polish them and check all the binding bolts for loosening.

Then all you need is your board, your gear and some snow before you can head off to enjoy another exhilarating season on the slopes.

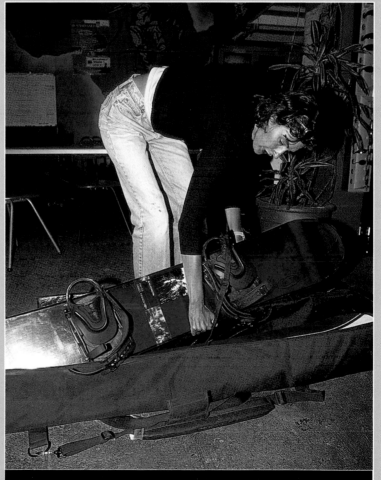

BOARD BAGS ARE NOTJUST GREAT FOR TRAVEL — THEY ALSO KEEP YOUR BOARD CLEAN AND DRY DURING OFF-SEASON STORAGE.

Clothing and Accessories

a newcomer to the sport might be forgiven for thinking that style alone dictates the snowboarder's dress code. But, as with most things, looks are not everything — the best snowboard-specific clothing is designed with function in mind. Comfort is a vital aspect; this means non-restrictive clothing that allows for a full range of movement, while still keeping the body warm and dry.

Knowing how to take advantage of a layering process to keep yourself adequately insulated is just as important as comfort. (A wet behind or frozen fingers will quickly put a damper on even the hardiest spirit.)

Choosing the right clothing will ensure that you are able to enjoy your snowboarding and make the best use of your precious time on the slopes, instead of desperately trying to thaw out inside the lodge.

Outerwear

Snowboarding requires the use of the entire body, not just the hips and legs, and well-designed clothing takes this physical mobility into consideration. Look for loose clothing — a little extra room allows for freedom of movement, while baggier jackets and trousers provide plenty of room for insulating layers underneath.

Extra length in the jacket prevents your midriff from coming into contact with snow when riding powder or taking a dramatic tumble. However, don't take the baggy look too far as oversized clothing could hinder you. It's better to stick with much the same clothing sizes you would normally choose. Quality outerwear for activities such as snowboarding is designed to keep the elements out while allowing excess moisture

generated by body heat to be 'wicked' away from the skin. The 'wicking' process insulates your body from external cold, wind and moisture, while maintaining self-generated body heat and removing any perspiration from your skin.

Fabric types

Fabrics that 'breathe' are usually synthetic or nylon-based, and are treated with a polyurethane coating. The better brands feature synthetics which actually facilitate the 'wicking' process, and are both practical and comfortable to wear. Snowboarders — particularly

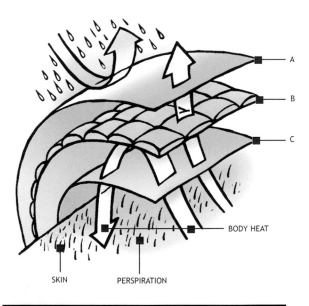

SKIN PERSPIRATION BODY HEAT

diagram HOW LAYERING PROVIDES INSULATION
A OUTER LAYER: WATERPROOF, BREATHABLE SHELL LAYER REPELS COLD AND MOISTURE.
B MIDDLE LAYER: SYNTHETIC OR WOOL TROUSERS AND SHIRT, FOLLOWED WITH FLEECE JACKET (OR VEST) AND TROUSERS ADD EXTRA INSULATION.
C INNER LAYER: POLYPROPYLENE SHIRT AND LEGGINGS 'WICK' MOISTURE AWAY FROM THE SKIN AND KEEP IT DRY.

opposite SNOWBOARD CLOTHING MUST BE DURABLE, COMFORTABLE AND FUNCTIONAL TO PROTECT RIDERS FROM THE ELEMENTS AND ALLOW FREEDOM OF MOVEMENT.

INNER THERMAL LAYER: This is the first layer of clothing that comes next to the skin . It should cover you from head to toe and comprises a long-sleeved top, socks and full-length leggings (long johns).

■ The inner thermal layer wicks excess moisture away from the skin and protects the body from chill by keeping it dry. It also serves to conserve body heat and keep the rider warm.

■ Synthetic materials (e.g. polypropylene) are the most effective for this purpose. However, avoid cotton garments — once they get wet, their insulation capacities are lost. Because they also absorb water, they might actually make you colder.

MIDDLE LAYER: This consists of two sub-layers; namely a lightweight synthetic or wool garment worn under a fleece jacket or vest, and trousers.

■ These layers add insulation by trapping body heat. Fleece is a good choice as it is able to 'breathe'. It therefore acts as an effective conduit for drawing moisture towards the outer layer of clothing.

■ When you want to shed a layer in warm weather conditions, choose the woollen or light synthetic one. As with the inner thermal layer, you should avoid wearing cotton garments at all costs.

OUTER SHELL LAYER: This 'shell' consists of synthetic fabric designed to keep moisture from snow out and protect you against the elements while still letting heat from perspiration escape. The shell layer should comprise a waterproof and windproof shell jacket and trousers. You should never underestimate the wind chill factor, as even a mild breeze can rapidly reduce your body temperature.

■ Be sure to choose a breathable fabric for outer shell clothing to ensure adequate protection from snow, wind and rain.

■ The ability of the outer layer to 'breathe' is important because it expels excess damp which has been transferred from the inner layers of clothing.

■ Many outfits feature zippered vents which assist this process by letting excess heat and moisture escape between runs or while you're relaxing.

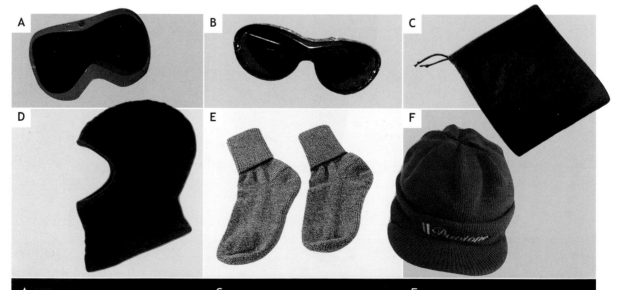

A GOOD QUALITY GOGGLES INCREASE VISIBILITY AND PROTECT YOUR FACE AND EYES.
B POLARIZED SUNGLASSES CAN BE WORN INSTEAD OF GOGGLES IN MILD WEATHER.

C FLEECE NECKWARMERS KEEP SNOW OUT.
D BALACLAVAS INSULATE THE HEAD AND NECK.
E THIN SYNTHETIC-BASED SOCKS KEEP FEET WARM AND DRY.

F FLEECE HATS ARE COMFORTABLE AND PROVIDE ITCH-FREE WARMTH. THEY ARE ALSO SUITABLE FOR ADDED PROTECTION IN EXTREME WEATHER CONDITIONS.

Last — but not least — are several other key components which should always be on your snowboarding clothing list. These are not merely luxuries or optional accessories, so don't go riding without them.

GLOVES are vital apparel for any snow sport and should be made of strong, durable material. They also help to shield the rider's hands from cold and wet conditions. Choose waterproof snowboarding gloves that have fleece or other synthetic-based insulated glove liners (usually removable for easy drying), in combination with nylon shell mittens or gloves. If you suffer from cold hands mittens provide better insulation than gloves.
■ Most gloves extend to the mid-forearm to keep snow out and some even incorporate drawstrings for added protection.
■ Choose gloves with built-in reinforcements of the palm and the undersides of the fingers as they keep these areas from wearing through.

A HAT helps retain body heat and protect your head from the elements, but a HELMET is a wiser choice - it will also retain heat, provide superior ventilation and moisture wicking, and of course protect your head from impact and possible injury. For more information on helmets, see 'Safety Equipment' on pg. 74.

WEARING GOOD PROTECTIVE CLOTHING IS AS IMPORTANT AS USING THE RIGHT EQUIPMENT TO ENSURE YOUR RIDE IS SAFE AND COMFORTABLE.

SOCKS are essential for keeping the feet warm, dry and comfortable.
■ Remember that soft boots incorporate some insulation, so thin, synthetic socks are a good choice.
■ Super-thick socks encourage feet to sweat and lose warmth more quickly.

GOGGLES protect the eyes from damaging ultraviolet (UV) rays while reducing the amount of glare that is reflected from the snow on sunny days.
■ In snowy conditions, goggles also protect the eyes from driving snow and enhance overall visibility.
■ As they cover most of the face, they offer good protection from sun- and wind-burn.
■ If goggles make you feel claustrophobic, rather choose a pair of good quality polarized sunglasses that filter out 100 per cent of harmful UVB rays.

A NECK WARMER can be pulled up over the lower half of the face for added protection in very cold and/or windy conditions.

Purchasing pointers

■ Don't just go by looks or price tags, as these are not always reliable guides to quality.
■ Read labels, and check the materials used. Ask sales staff for advice if you're unsure.
■ Ensure that outerwear is really waterproof — if it requires additional waterproofing treatment, it is probably not the best choice.
■ Also check for high-quality stitching and workmanship, and reinforced seams on clothing items.
■ And finally, always try on clothes before you buy.

Getting Started

In the early days of snowboarding, beginners battled to learn how to ride a board. When this adventure sport was still in its infancy, there just weren't many experts out there and few resorts had established any form of snowboarding curriculum. New riders simply had to strap on their boards and challenge the snow, equipped, at best, with a couple of pointers from other snowboarding enthusiasts.

Fortunately, those pioneer riders persevered and snowboarding flourished. Today's scenario is much brighter, with most snowboard-friendly resorts offering accredited schools and professionally trained instructors. This means that learning to ride has become more fun and also much safer.

One of the main attractions of snowboarding — other than the fact that it is an exhilarating adventure sport — is the learning curve. Most instructors will tell you that it only takes about three days to learn the basic skills you need to ride. The biggest obstacle in the way of most beginners is committing to moving on the board before they know exactly how to control it. Surprisingly, the board is actually a lot easier to handle when it is moving.

Once you've gained confidence by sliding on the board's base, you can begin learning to use the edges to traverse. Then it's time for various edging moves. After you've learnt the basic manoeuvres, you'll be ready for linking the toeside and heelside turns, which are important skills in snowboarding.

You will be amazed at just how easy it is to master the basics. Don't become discouraged by spills. Keep in mind the short span of time it will take you to master techniques that will equip you to face the challenge of varying types of terrain, all over the mountain.

opposite PRACTISING THE BASICS, LIKE STOPPING THE BOARD BY SIDE-SLIPPING HEELSIDE, WILL HELP YOU GAIN CONFIDENCE.

Be humble and take lessons

Do yourself a favour, save time and energy and take lessons. Most resort snowboard schools make it easy for you, offering comprehensive beginners deals which include a lesson, lift pass and all the equipment you need, at very reasonable prices. Some rental packages even include items like knee and butt pads to make your first few unexpected landings safer. It is essential that you learn proper techniques right from the beginning. Think of it as a recording process: when you make that first turn correctly, your mind is imprinted. It 'records' the movement, allowing you to 'play it back' when you try to repeat the manoeuvre. If you start by teaching yourself and allow incorrect techniques to become ingrained, you'll have 'recorded' bad habits that will later have to be 'erased' before you can learn the correct methods. A qualified instructor will quickly ascertain your level of ability and the amount of coaching you'll need. He or she will be able to answer any questions you may have, and make sure that you start your snowboarding experience as you mean to continue, the right way.

The importance of warming up and stretching

Whether you are a beginner or not, it is important to get your muscles ready for a day's riding, and that means, at the very least, a quick warm-up and stretch.

This will enhance your overall riding performance and greatly reduce your chances of pulling a muscle. You need to increase your heart rate and get your circulation flowing to pump blood to your leg muscles. Take a brisk walk around the lodge or tackle a few sets of stairs then do some basic quadriceps, hamstring and calf stretches before strapping on your board (see pp 75-77). Many people even take a slow and easy warm-up run at the beginning of the day, then stop to stretch out a bit more before continuing to ride.

Stance: regular or 'goofy'

BEFORE TAKING YOUR FIRST foray you'll need to establish the most natural stance position which feels relaxed and comfortable for you. Your front foot is the one you'll need to commit your weight to, in order to make the board go downhill, so it is essential to determine which foot feels most comfortable in the forward position on the board. Even expert snowboarders who are equally at ease riding forward or fakie tend to have their own natural stance preference.

Your stance on a snowboard is either regular or what riders term 'goofy'. These terms, borrowed from surfing and skateboarding jargon, simply describe which stance you prefer. 'Regular' riders ride with their left foot forward, while 'goofy' riders ride with their right foot forward.

Finding out which stance comes naturally to you from the very beginning will save you a lot of time and frustration later on. If you have lessons without taking your natural stance into

consideration, you may be attempting to learn with the wrong foot forward, which will make it unnecessarily difficult and frustrating for you.

Some people — especially those who surf or skateboard — will already have their own preference. If you are unsure, the simplest and most commonly used method for finding out is to take a slide across a smooth surface, like a hardwood floor, in your socks and see which foot you are naturally inclined to put first.

A

B

RIGHT FOOT
FORWARD

LEFT FOOT
FORWARD

WHETHER YOU ARE REGULAR OR 'GOOFY', TEST TO MAKE SURE YOU'RE USING THE STANCE THAT FEELS NATURAL TO YOU.

A REGULAR STANCE MEANS YOUR LEFT FOOT IS FORWARD.   B IF YOU'RE 'GOOFY', YOU RIDE WITH YOUR RIGHT FOOT FORWARD.

ONCE YOU'VE DECIDED ON A regular or goofy direction and set up your bindings accordingly (see pp 23-25) you are ready to start practising a proper riding stance on a flat surface.

■ Your basic stance is the neutral position from which all your other movements will be made, which is why it's so important to get it right before even starting to learn. You may even want to get a head start by strapping on your board at home and becoming familiar with the basic movements before you head for the slopes.

■ Once on the board, your knees should be slightly bent as with any good athletic stance. Be careful not to strain your quadricep muscles, but bend them just enough to lower your centre of gravity slightly, to improve your balance.

■ The forward lean on your bindings' highbacks should, if properly adjusted, indicate the amount of knee bend you should be practising on your board.

■ Your weight should be evenly distributed over both legs, but should be slightly more concentrated on the forward leg.

■ Keep your upper body erect with your head up and facing forward, and your arms and hands relaxed at your sides.

■ Remember: snowboarding involves continual movement, so it's easier if you try to stay loose and relaxed, not rigid.

A
WRONG STANCE
TOO MUCH
BACKWARD LEAN

B
CORRECT STANCE
WITH WEIGHT
CENTRED

C
WRONG STANCE -
TOO FAR FORWARD

A INCORRECT RIDING STANCE SHOWING TOO MUCH BACKWARD LEAN.

B THE CORRECT STANCE WITH WEIGHT PERFECTLY CENTRED ENSURES BALANCE.

C INCORRECT STANCE WITH TOO MUCH FORWARD LEAN.

Strapping in, standing up

When you're ready to strap in (see sequence below), put your board down on a level patch of snow and sit down so that the board is out in front of you with the heelside edge facing toward you.

First snap your safety leash on around the calf of your front leg to keep the board from getting away from you (A), then brush any accumulated snow out of the bindings and off the bottom of your boots. Start by first buckling in your front foot. Place your foot into the binding, then ratchet down the ankle strap, tightly enough so that your boot nestles securely into the heel cup. Once the ankle strap is fastened, secure the toe strap (B). If your bindings have a third strap for the lower calf, fasten this one last. Repeat this process with your back foot, until both are fully strapped in (C). Now you are ready to stand up (D).

To get into a standing position, first roll over onto your knees by kicking your board up with your front foot (E). Then twist your body until you roll over onto your hands and knees with the board's toeside edge down (F). Once you have done this, use your hands to gradually 'walk' yourself into an upright position with both your knees bent (G), then push with your hands until you are able to stand up straight (H). Now you are ready to learn how to move on flat ground.

■ Both feet should only be buckled in once you are at the top of a hill, ready to ride.

THE BASICS OF STRAPPING IN AND STANDING UP ARE EASY ONCE YOU KNOW HOW.

When buckling in at the base of the mountain to head toward the lift, always leave your back foot free. This ensures that you will be able to traverse flat sections by skating.

Skating

'Skating' the board from one place to another is a handy skill that you will need to master. You will have to skate when you are making a mid-mountain transfer from lift to lift, when crossing the flats from the base lodge over to a lift or when trying to get moving again if you get caught on a 'cat track' (a flat spot without enough incline to keep you in motion). Though it may seem clumsy at first, skating is much more efficient than unstrapping the board and walking. Practising this useful technique will also help you to get the feel of gliding the board forward on the flat before you attempt the same motion on a gradual slope.

Starting to skate

■ Strap your front foot into its binding, leaving your back foot free. Try this in a quiet, level spot, away from the crowds.

■ With your weight balanced on your front foot, push yourself forward with your back foot, just as you would on a skateboard or scooter.

■ Start with very short steps and gradually work up, keeping in mind that you should never plant your free foot further ahead than your front (strapped) foot.

■ Once you feel comfortable with the movements, try gliding further by pushing off with your free foot, then placing it on the board's stomp pad, and riding out the momentum until you stop completely.

Gliding downhill

Once you feel confident utilizing your board's base and gliding on a flat surface, you will be ready to try it out for a short distance on a small slope. Gliding downhill is your first attempt at downhill snowboarding and is done with both feet, front foot buckled in and the back foot resting on the board's stomp pad. Performing a basic forward downhill glide will help you to gain control and build confidence in committing your weight to downhill movement. This is especially important when you begin learning how to use the board's edges to control your direction of travel.

skating SKATING MAY SEEM CLUMSY, BUT IT GETS YOU FROM ONE PLACE TO ANOTHER.

gliding PRACTISE GLIDING ON THE FLATS BEFORE YOU ATTEMPT IT ON A SMALL SLOPE.

climbing WHEN CLIMBING IT'S IMPORTANT TO KEEP THE BOARD STRAIGHT ACROSS THE HILL.

The fall line

ALTHOUGH SOME BEGINNERS have a skiing or other snow sports background, not all snowboarders get their start crossing over from other disciplines. If you are not familiar with snow-covered slopes don't worry; you will gain experience very quickly once you start.

In the early stages, it is important to have a working knowledge of the fall line, an imaginary line that cuts straight down the steepest part of a slope. This is the natural path that gravity will take an object rolling (or in your case sliding) down it. Take a snowball, for instance, and roll it down any given slope — the path it takes will be directly along the fall line. Since slopes can have many different contours, bear in mind that the fall line is not necessarily always straight down the middle of the hill.

Why is this knowledge important in snowboarding? Since all basic snowboarding movements relate to the fall line, understanding the fall line principle will keep you in control as you begin to learn to use your board's edges.

The rule of thumb is as follows:
■ The more parallel to the fall line your board's position, the *faster* you will go.
■ The more perpendicular it is, the *slower* you will move.
■ If your snowboard is perfectly perpendicular across the fall line, you will come to a complete stop on the slope.

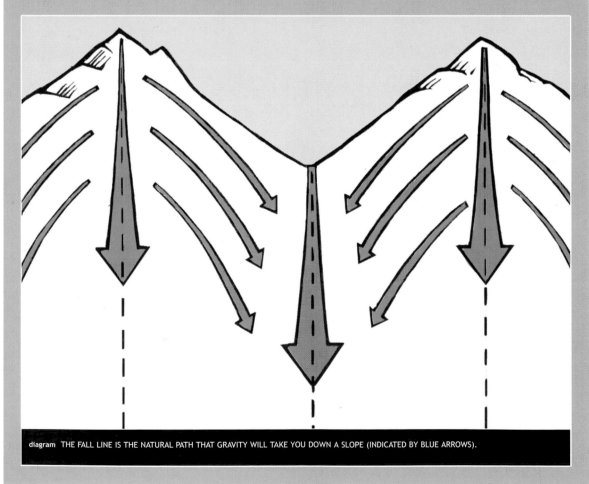

diagram THE FALL LINE IS THE NATURAL PATH THAT GRAVITY WILL TAKE YOU DOWN A SLOPE (INDICATED BY BLUE ARROWS).

Climbing

Climbing is a useful method for hiking a small uphill stretch while leaving your front foot buckled in.

■ First, make sure you are on a very gradual beginner's slope with plenty of level ground below for runout space. Hike up the slope by sidestepping, which is done as follows:

■ Facing the hill — with your front foot buckled in and your back foot free — place the board across the downhill slope.

■ Step up with your free foot, then follow with the board, taking small steps and keeping the board straight across the slope.

■ Kick the board's toeside edge into the snow for traction at each step. Don't go too high up initially — remember, you are going to be riding down for the first time — so do not be too ambitious.

■ With your weight resting on your free foot, lift your board up, then point the nose directly downhill, and rest the board on the snow. Make sure you keep your weight on the free foot.

■ When you're ready, transfer your weight to your front foot as you lift your free foot and rest it on the board's stomp pad. The weight on your front foot will set the board in motion, and gravity will do the rest.

■ Once in motion, keep your stance as relaxed as possible, with your weight on your front foot; if you shift your weight toward the back foot, you are likely to lose control and take a spill. Run this movement all the way to the flat, then turn around and try again, gradually climbing higher with each try as you gain more confidence on the board.

Toeside and heelside stopping

Now that you are comfortable performing a straight glide on a gradual slope, it is time to put your new-found knowledge of the fall line to work when you learn to stop by making use of the edges of the board. Remember that you will not be riding on the 'bunny hill' or beginner's slope for very long. So, learning how to stop using either edge is a skill that cannot be overemphasized, particularly when you begin riding on more challenging terrain.

A STOPPING USING THE HEELSIDE (UPHILL) EDGE.
B STOPPING USING THE TOESIDE EDGE.

Falling follies

Falling is every beginner's worst nightmare but it is, unfortunately, a necessary part of the learning process to a greater or lesser degree.

The most common reason for falling in the early stages is catching the downhill edge and falling forward; the edge gets gripped by the snow which takes you unawares and causes you to land heavily on your hands and knees. You can minimize or even eliminate falls by remembering a very simple rule: always keep your downhill edge up and out of the snow.

Luckily, there are plenty of safeguards available to cushion the blows you may experience on your first few turns; knee pads, padded suit-pants and wrist guards are available from most rental shops and could prevent a few spectacular bruises.

When you do fall, try your best to stay relaxed and allow yourself to roll with it. If you fall forward, your natural reflex will be to put your hands out to stop the fall. Avoid this at all costs.

If you fall forward, bring your hands in towards the sternum and fall on your forearms to minimize any potential wrist injury. If you try to stop yourself with your arms or palms extended you could injure yourself.

Falling backward is almost always due to loss of control that causes your board to speed up and slip out from under you. If you feel yourself falling backward, try to turn the board uphill to slow yourself down. Lead your backward fall with your rear (as if you were trying to sit), and try to roll with the fall.

Moreover, this introductory edging practice will really come in handy when you start learning how to traverse and turn.

■ Start just as you did when practising the gliding manoeuvre; choose a similar, quiet, gradual slope and hike up again by sidestepping.

■ Again, once you are at the top keep the rear foot unstrapped and firmly planted in the snow with your weight balanced on it.

■ Point your board downhill and repeat the gliding exercise just as before, shifting your weight onto your front foot while stepping with your rear foot onto the stomp pad.

■ Now, instead of riding your momentum out to the bottom of the hill, practise a controlled toeside stop about mid-way down the slope.

■ To initiate the stop, gradually shift your weight onto your toes and then balance the board on the toeside edge.

■ As you begin to edge, use your back foot to push the tail end of the board gently downhill so that the board moves in an arc until it is perpendicular to the fall line. Make sure you stay balanced on the toeside edge until you complete the stop.

■ Next, try stopping in the other direction by initiating a heelside stop. Begin as you did before, this time, balancing your weight on the heelside edge, while simultaneously pushing the tail end of the board downhill.

■ Keep the downhill (toeside) edge up and out of the snow. Stay on the uphill edge as you arc the board until it is perpendicular to the fall line.

Sideslipping

A sideslip is a controlled sideways slide along the fall line of a slope — snowboarding's version of the skier's snowplough. Mastering the sideslip is essential because it will allow you to bypass any difficult terrain with ease. It is not just a beginner's move — someday when you have to descend a steep run, you'll be glad to have the sideslip as an option.

Controlled sideslipping is important to the learning process because it familiarizes you with the toeside and heelside edge control you need to learn in order to traverse, and eventually to perform basic turns. Sideslipping entails increasing and decreasing the angle of your board's uphill edge according to the slope — decreasing the angle initiates the sliding movement, while increasing the edge angle slows the board down and brings it to a stop. A useful tip to remember is to always keep your downhill edge of the board up and out of the snow.

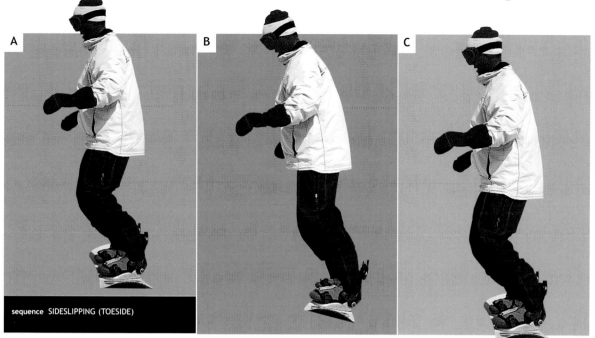

sequence SIDESLIPPING (TOESIDE)

Sideslipping (toeside)

Begin on a moderate slope with both feet strapped in, facing uphill with your board directly across the fall line (see sequence above). Bend your knees with your weight evenly distributed over both legs, and you balance on your uphill (toeside) edge (A).

Gently reduce the board's edge angle to begin sliding directly downhill along the fall line (B). Increase the board's edge angle to slow down and stop (C). Practise this down the slope and try performing controlled sideslips at gradually longer intervals until you can easily control the length and speed of the sideslip.

sequence SIDESLIPPING (HEELSIDE)

Sideslipping (heelside)

To practise the same manoeuvre heelside (see previous page), turn right around and begin just as you did before, with the board across the fall line, but now balancing on your uphill (heelside) edge (A). Again, reduce the board's edge angle by pushing down on your toes (B). Increase the angle of the heelside edge by lifting the toeside edge (C). Just as you did with the toeside sideslip, practise this at gradually longer intervals, focusing on controlling the length and speed.

You should have the sideslip mastered in no time. Use this move whenever necessary, but try not to rely on it completely. If you find yourself needing to sideslip the entire length of a run in order to get down, chances are that you are trying to ride terrain that is just beyond your current capabilities.

Traversing

When you feel comfortable with sideslipping, you can begin working on toeside and heelside traverses. To traverse a trail means to tack back and forth across its width, zigzagging diagonally across the fall line. Mastery of this skill gives you control over your speed and direction, and will further familiarize you with the balancing and edging techniques you'll need to learn the basic turn. Another advantage is that you no longer have to ride straight down the slope.

Toeside traverse

When you start with a toeside traverse (see sequence below), your body will be facing uphill, your weight even over both feet and balanced on the uphill (toeside) edge, and the board will be perpendicular across the fall line. Start moving with a toeside sideslip, then shift your weight onto your front foot and turn your head and torso to face the direction you want to travel towards (A). Traverse across the entire width of the slope, travelling very slightly downhill and keeping your toeside edge engaged with the downhill edge up and out of the snow (B). When you reach the far end of the trail, stop by turning the board uphill and directly across the fall line (C). Once you come to a complete stop, rest on your knees and flip round. Now you are ready to traverse in the opposite direction using the heelside edge.

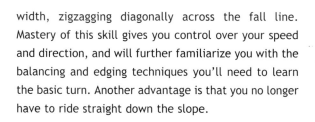

sequence WHEN DOING TOESIDE TRAVERSE KEEP YOUR HEAD AND TORSO FACING FORWARD AND STAY ON YOUR UPHILL EDGE.

A   B   C

A B C

Heelside traverse

Start with the board resting on the uphill (heelside) edge (see sequence above), directly across the fall line. Begin sideslipping heelside, then transfer your weight to the front foot to begin traversing (A). Again, turn your head and torso in the direction you are travelling and keep the board angled just slightly downhill (B). Stop on your heelside edge by returning the board to its original position directly across the fall line (C). When you come to a stop, sit down, flip round and repeat the toeside traverse, continuing back and forth across the trail until you reach the bottom. Keep practising this until you feel comfortable traversing, controlling both edges, and you are confident that you can make a controlled stop whenever necessary.

The 'falling leaf'

Once you know how to make controlled traverses on both edges, the next manoeuvre you need to learn is known as the 'falling leaf'. This is similar to traversing but it incorporates a direction change, with your first experience of riding 'fakie' or tail end first. As you tra-

verse back and forth across the fall line while remaining on the same edge, the motion that you'll make is similar to that of a gently falling leaf. Learning how to do the 'falling leaf' hones your edging control skills without committing you (as yet) to edge-to-edge changes. Furthermore, it will allow you to travel in any direction regardless of which way your board is facing. Riding 'fakie' is actually the first freestyle manoeuvre one learns in snowboarding. It will be useful later, when you begin to experiment with more advanced freestyle riding. To begin with, the toeside falling leaf (see sequence p48). Start as you would when performing a toeside traverse, by putting weight on your front foot and cutting across the trail's fall line while keeping your balance on the toeside or uphill edge (A). Remember to keep the traversing angle very slight. Once you get to the far end of the trail, stop, as you would in a traverse, by bringing the board back to an angle directly across the fall line (B).

sequence FALLING LEAF (TOESIDE).

This is where the change begins: instead of flipping over and beginning a heelside traverse on the other edge, stay balanced on your toeside edge, turn your head and look over your shoulder. Then gently shift your weight backward onto your rear foot (now your leading foot) and traverse back across the trail 'fakie' (C). Remember to keep your angle very slight and make sure you stay on the toeside edge. Once you reach the opposite end of the trail, shift your weight and direction again (D), and continue with another toeside traverse, once again riding the board nose-first (E).

Once you have completed a few of these on the toeside edge, switch to the heelside edge and repeat the exercise. Remember to keep your downhill angle slight, look in the direction in which you want to go and maintain that uphill edge.

As you become more adept at the falling leaf on either edge, try controlling your traverses while moving progressively faster. Also try making shorter traverses once you're comfortable traversing the entire length of the trail or try to traverse only half-way across.

Garlands

After learning to traverse, sideslip and reinforce your edging abilities with the falling leaf, garlands are the last step before tackling basic, linked turns.

Though they only make use of one edge at a time, garlands are actually linked turns (though not complete turns) that allow you to travel downhill in controlled, fluid movements. They represent a step forward from simple traversing to actual turning. Once you have this partial-turning manoeuvre down to a fine art, it will be much easier to make the transition to the full edge-to-edge turning technique. Practise this technique on a wide slope far away from large groups.

Start with a heelside traverse, (see sequence below) exactly the same as before, except that you must adopt a slightly more downhill traversing angle. Weight your front foot and travel heelside until you begin to build up speed (A).

Perform the garland turn by arcing the board toward a position across the fall line, but stopping short of a complete turn by weighting your front foot again and continuing on the downhill traverse (B). Concentrate on making a controlled, arcing movement across the fall line, not a braking stop.

Your head and torso should be turned in the direction in which you're travelling, but the majority of the turn should stem from lower body movement.

Initiate the turn by turning your leading foot uphill and pushing the board's tail through the arc with your rear foot.

Try to continue across the slope in fluid, controlled movements, without coming to a complete stop until you reach the far side of the trail (C). Once you have completed this series of turns, practise going in the opposite direction across the trail by performing garlands on the heelside edge.

When you feel comfortable performing this manoeuvre on either edge, make your downhill angle a little steeper to increase your speed. Also, practise making the garlands at varying intervals — from closer together to wider apart — until you can perform them on demand, on either edge and under control.

sequence ONCE YOU'VE MASTERED GARLAND TURNS IT WON'T BE LONG BEFORE YOU ARE MAKING FULL TURNS ACROSS THE FALL LINE.

At last — linked turns

Now that you are able to traverse on both edges and can control your speed when sideslipping, you are ready to take the final step — from performing partial turns across the fall line (as you did with garlands) to complete, edge-to-edge turns.

If this seems like a daunting task, consider this: having mastered traversing and garland turns, you've already completed two-thirds of the lesson.

Heelside and toeside traverses represent the beginning and ending positions of a turn, while garlands represent the initiation of the turn itself. Now, the last building block in this process is the ability to link these movements by completing the turn, and shifting from one edge to the other. With this final step in place, you will be able to control your speed and direction at all times.

Remember that timing is a key component of toeside and heelside turns. Time your shift from one edge to another as close to the fall line as possible. The momentum gained when the board is briefly pointed downhill will provide much of the energy needed for making the turn, and the distance between edges will be at its narrowest point, making the edge to edge shift easier.

To begin with, find a groomed, gradual slope with as little change in contour as possible. Also, choose an uncrowded area — you want to concentrate on your turns and the presence of other people will just make you nervous and distract you. If you can't find an empty area to practise in, wait for a lull in the downhill traffic.

Plan your attack before you take off. Analyze the run from the top, create an imaginary path to follow and make a mental note of where you might initiate your turns. Don't worry about being precise — this is just a guideline.

Most beginners find the toeside turn easier at first (see A and B in sequence below), so start with a heelside traverse, as before but at a steeper angle. If you need to, perform a garland as you traverse to keep yourself at a comfortable speed.

Remember — keep the knees bent, centre of gravity low — and turn your head and torso to face the direction you wish to travel towards. When you are ready, turn your head and torso to face the direction you want to turn to (A). Now, initiate the turn by shifting your weight forward to point the board downhill, twisting

sequence LINKED TURN (TOESIDE TO HEELSIDE).

A   B   C

your front foot to steer the board across the fall line and pushing the board through the turn with your rear foot (B). Remember to extend your legs and shift your weight upward as you cross the fall line. Ensure that you make a smooth edge change by rolling from one edge to the other. After you have changed edges (and direction), bend your knees to set the new uphill (toeside) edge, continue to face the direction you wish to go to, and make a long, steady traverse as you look out for your next turning point.

Now you are ready for the **heelside turn.** Once again, turn your head and torso in the direction of the turn, shift your weight forward, and initiate your turn as you extend your legs and roll onto the heelside edge (C). Then use your rear foot to push the board across the fall line and through the turn, bending your knees and setting the uphill (heelside) edge as you complete the turn (D).

Concentrate on linking these turns two at a time (one on each edge), then build until you have them under control, down the length of the practice slope (E,F). Remember to use your other skills (sideslipping, garlands, traverses) to stay in control. For instance, if

Helpful tips:

■ Shifting your weight upward by extending your legs as you initiate the turn makes the transition much easier.

■ Remember that your legs are doing the work; your upper body should stay straight and centred.

■ As you traverse on your uphill edge, keep your knees bent so your centre of gravity is low and your weight works for you to keep the edge set in the snow.

■ When you are ready to pivot and change edges, straightening your legs will release the edge, letting the board slide across the base to the other edge.

■ Once you have achieved the change of edge (and therefore of direction) bend your knees again to set the new edge.

■ This bending-and-extending method will also be useful as a shock absorber when you begin to experiment with different terrain and snow conditions.

you encounter a steep stretch of trail, sideslip past it until you come to a spot that you feel comfortable to turn on. Try shortening the intervals between turns as you gain proficiency.

sequence LINKED TURN (CONTINUED).

D E F

RESORTS OFTEN PROVIDE POMAS (also known as button lifts) and T-bars to access some of the area's most beginner-friendly terrain. However, since these lift types were not originally designed with snowboarders in mind, they can be a little tricky for riders to use.

T-bars and pomas are designed on the assumption that the user will be facing straight up the hill, legs side by side, and not facing sideways as in the snowboarding stance. Unlike skiers, who would grip the poma (button) between their legs, snowboarders usually just hold onto the poma or T-bar with their hands and get towed uphill that way. Rope tows work in a similar fashion — simply grab onto the rope and hold on till you reach the top.

Another potential hazard of these lifts for beginners is that you are required to steer the board straight all the way up the hill. This may be difficult to do if you're not comfortable with your edges yet. However, it is good practice in the long run. A chairlift is much easier for a beginner to handle than a T-bar or poma, so choose that option if possible.

Gondolas or cable cars are large, enclosed cabin lifts that can carry groups of skiers and riders. They are very easy and comfortable to travel on as you simply walk on and off, carrying your board. Bear in mind that gondolas normally access terrain high up on the mountain that is unsuitable for beginners. Make sure you are not getting in over your head before you board the tram — or you may have to ride right back down again.

Your first time

Chances are you're at least a little nervous about riding the chairlift for the first time. The thought of making a rookie blunder — especially in plain view of a line of people — does not sound like much fun.

The truth is that there is really nothing to it. Getting on and off the chairlift is only a

A GONDOLA LIFTS CAN COMFORTABLY ACCOMMODATE LARGE GROUPS OF SNOWBOARDERS OR SKIERS.

B POMA LIFT.

C T-BAR LIFT.

matter of utilizing three basic skills that you will have mastered by the time you take the lifts: skating, gliding and making a controlled stop. The reason chairlift manoeuvres strike terror into raw recruits is that the lifts keep moving on a controlled loop, so there is not much room for error. However, you will find that experienced and kindly lift attendant will work wonders.

Using the chair-lift

■ With just your front foot strapped in, enter the line for the chairlift and skate through until you reach the point just before the loading area, which is marked by a line and a sign instructing you to 'Stop Here'.

■ Once you arrive at this point, make sure the lift attendant knows that you're a beginner so he can slow the lift down for you and make your first attempt easier. Also, if you are boarding the chairlift with strangers, it is a good idea to alert them too.

■ When the group in front of you gets onto the lift (and when the lift attendant tells you it is okay to go), skate onto the loading area and stop at the take-off spot. Again, this is clearly marked with a line across the platform.

■ Immediately after you reach the take-off point, look over

your shoulder and reach backwards with one hand to grab the oncoming chair and to stabilize yourself.

■ As the chair reaches the point just before it makes contact with the backs of your knees, sit down and you're away.

Riding the chair

As soon as you are settled in the chair, lower the safety bar if there is one. It will seem awkward and a little uncomfortable to have your board dangling at first, so take some of the pressure off your front foot by hooking your free foot under the tail of the board.

■ Then sit back and enjoy the view, pick up tips by watching other riders descending the slopes and keep a look out for stretches of terrain that you might want to try out on your way down.

Unloading — getting off the chair lift

■ When you begin to approach the unloading area (usually marked with a 'Prepare to Unload' sign), unhook your back foot and raise the safety bar.

■ Point your board forward and keep the nose pointing upward. It may help you to pivot your body sideways in the chair.

■ When you reach the unloading point, rest your back

RIDING THE CHAIRLIFT IS NOT AS DIFFICULT AS IT LOOKS AND MOST SNOW RESORTS HAVE HELPFUL LIFT ATTENDANTS.

foot on the stomp pad before you set the board down.

■ Set the board's tail down first, then stand up and glide down the off-ramp just as you did when practising the forward glide.

■ There is usually enough run-out space at the bottom of the ramp, but if there isn't, you may need to perform a controlled stop.

■ Once you have come to a complete stop, quickly move away from the unloading area.

■ The last thing you want before you even start riding is to collide with people getting off the chair right behind you.

Advanced Skills

by now you will have mastered the basic turns and perhaps will have tentatively begun to explore fresh areas and new terrain all over the mountain. Learning to turn and ride down the slopes was your first goal but those basic skills just prepare you for the variety of thrills this exciting sport has to offer.

In addition to tackling terrain of increasing difficulty, you are now ready to branch out with confidence and explore some of the other disciplines found in snowboarding.

Freeriding allows you to experience the whole gamut of riding options by encouraging you to experiment with several riding styles simultaneously, while you gain all-mountain proficiency in a broad array of terrains and conditions.

Freestyle riding allows you to take to the air, perfecting tricks and 'airs' (jumps) in the halfpipe and terrain park. Becoming a **carving** enthusiast will increase your speed, style and grace, revealing the true essence of the turn. Learning about the different types of competition that are open to you will challenge you to extend your own limits by using your skills to challenge those of other riders. For those looking for a more extreme outdoor experience: the big backcountry snowfields await you.

Some riders choose to dabble in a few areas of every discipline, experiencing everything that snowboarding has to offer, while others find maximum satisfaction in becoming experts in a specific category of riding. Whichever direction beckons you — this is where the real fun of snowboarding begins.

Freeriding

This entails being an all-mountain rider, at home anywhere on the mountain. Most freeriders are happiest when threading a tree run or discovering trackless slopes of powder snow, but many still enjoy taking a few runs in a terrain park, and revel in the pleasure of carving a groomed corduroy run.

Freeriding is all about being versatile, knowing how to handle every sort of terrain under all kinds of conditions. If you think this is the way you'd like snowboarding to take you, you will need to adopt some specific riding skills to guide you in the direction of all-mountain proficiency.

Riding powder

For most snowboarders, riding powder is the essence of the sport — it simply doesn't get much better than surfing your way through soft, deep virgin snow and throwing up a thick white plume in your wake. After your first successful powder run, you'll probably become an addict. Soon you will find yourself anticipating perfect snow conditions, and even getting up early in the morning to claim those first few pristine powder runs for your own.

Once you are confident and comfortable with making linked turns on a groomed run, you are ready to begin experimenting with the thrills of riding powder. The most important thing to remember is to keep the nose of the board up and out of the snow, so that the board stays planing over the top of the powder. If the nose tilts down and gets buried, you and the board will follow it. Once the board sinks below the surface of the snow, you'll come to an abrupt halt. To keep the tip of the nose up, shift your weight back on your rear leg as you ride — this is a departure from the basic turn on groomed snow in which most of your weight is concentrated on the forward foot.

Getting up in powder

If you are able to ride powder regularly, sooner or later you're going to get stuck in some deep snow. Digging yourself out of this powdery predicament and getting moving again can initially be a little difficult, not to mention frustrating.

These pointers will reduce your downtime considerably:

■ When you take a spill or get stuck, get up on your toeside — it is easier to stand up from a kneeling position than from being flat on your behind. If the board is deeply buried you may have to dig yourself out with your hands.

■ In some cases, it's easier to get the board back onto the surface by unstrapping your rear foot and then dragging the board out.

■ NEVER release both feet and the leash in deep snow. For one thing, you could lose your board under the surface of the snow. Alternatively, if you happen to let go of your board once it is on the surface again, you could let yourself in for a time-consuming and frustrating experience retrieving it if it takes off downhill. There is always the chance that the rogue board may have a damaging encounter with a fellow-snowboarder or an unwary skier, with dire consequences.

■ Although it may seem easier to hike a few feet before starting to ride again, it's better to try riding out from a stop in deeper snow. Powder is often deep, and your feet are likely to sink quite far before you encounter solid snow. This potentially exhausting predicament, known as 'post-holing', is a waste of energy. The best advice is to rather stay where you fell, get your board up above the surface and strapped on again, and then begin moving downhill from there.

LEARNING TO RIDE IN DEEP UNTRACKED POWDER SNOW TAKES PRACTICE AND SHOULD ONLY BE ATTEMPTED ONCE YOU ARE CONFIDENT.

You will notice at once that riding powder takes much more lower-body strength. Your rear leg will not only be supporting most of your weight, it will also be instrumental in pushing you through your turns. Changing your stance setup can make this much easier for you; if it has been snowing hard the night before and you know you can look forward to a day of powder riding, try shifting the bindings back towards the rear of the board's hole pattern. Your back leg muscles will thank you for it later.

Also, keep in mind that you will need to point your board straighter down the fall line than you would normally do on a groomed run. Deep powder can actually slow you down a bit, so maximize your speed and keep yourself from stalling out and getting stuck.

The deeper the snow, the straighter you must aim down the fall line. Head straight down a steep section if you can see that the run flattens out a bit ahead; you will need the extra momentum to carry you through the flat and keep you from getting bogged down.

Finally, remember the 'rising and falling' motion you learned to create by bending and extending your legs through your basic turns; this rhythmic motion is an integral part of powder riding. As soon as there is a day of deep powder snow ahead, find a run that you feel comfortable with, and start to practise.

Head straight down the fall line at first, gaining momentum as you transfer your weight back onto your rear leg. Keep your rear knee flexed and your front knee straighter. This helps to keep the board's nose above the snow. Initiate turns just as you would on a groomed run, but stay parallel to the fall line.

Remember to maintain a low centre of gravity when going into a turn, and spring upwards, by extending your legs slightly to stay above the snow, as you make the edge change. You should be able to feel the board sinking slightly into the snow as you begin to turn, then rising up over it as you extend your legs. Keep your upper body straight, let your legs do the work, and remember — above all — keep the nose of the board up.

As you develop more confidence (and build up extra strength in your legs) try some steeper runs, with deeper snow, whenever possible. Soon your biggest challenge won't be how to ride powder, but how to find a pristine powder slope before everyone else does.

Finding powder

Virgin powder is snowboarding's most precious commodity — and it usually does not stay track-free for long. To make sure you get your fair share of the 'freshies' (freshly fallen show), ride early. If it has snowed hard the previous night and you know there will be powder on the slopes, try to ensure that you are among the first waiting in line when the lift opens in the morning, or as close as you can get.

Riding off-piste (off the marked, groomed run) is also a good way to find powder when the marked trails (on-piste areas) are full of old tracks. Another great place to look for deep snow is along the sides of your

WHEN RIDING THROUGH TREES, USE POWDER TO SLOW YOU DOWN QUICKLY BY RIDING INTO A SECTION OF DEEP POWDER AND THEN TURNING.

favourite runs; as they get full of tracks during the course of the day, snow gets pushed to the edges of the trails. Ride along the fringes of the runs and you'll be sure to find some snow that is relatively deeper, and (if you are lucky) still trackless. Remember that obstacles such as holes and buried rocks may be hidden beneath deep powder, so be on the lookout.

Riding through the trees

Riding off-piste through tree runs can be one of the most enjoyable aspects of the freeriding experience. Riders with local knowledge try to keep their favourite wooded places secret, and with good reason; these spots are usually some of the most peaceful and aesthetically pleasing areas to be found. They also often conceal treasure troves of deep, trackless snow.

A big plus is that tree runs provide blissful solitude when the on-piste terrain is hectically crowded. Riding through silent, snow-covered pine-scented trees is a special thrill. To top it all, there is nothing like blasting powder turns while navigating your own trail through a natural maze to get a tidal wave of adrenaline flowing.

As exhilarating and challenging as tree riding may be, it is not entirely without its pitfalls. Knowing how to approach this type of terrain will ensure that you stay out of danger while you have your fun.

Riding in different conditions

Naturally all riders would be delighted if every day on the slopes could be a picture-perfect powder day with peak conditions. But, as with any outdoor activity that depends on the weather, some days will be more conducive to riding pleasure than others.

Instead of treating icy or wet snow conditions as negatives, view them as challenges that will hone your overall riding skills and give you the necessary experience for all-mountain riding.

These tips will help you adapt your riding skills for adverse snow conditions:

Wet snow
Riding in wet snow is a drag — quite literally. The resistance created by wet, heavy snow will bog you down quickly if you are not prepared for it. The feel of riding in wet snow is a far cry from riding powder, but treat these two snow conditions the same.

■ Do not complete your turns as neatly as you would in average conditions, as this will only reduce your speed.

NO ONE LIKES CROSSING AN ICE PATCH — OPT FOR SIDESLIPPING AND KEEP YOUR BALANCE BY MINIMIZING YOUR MOVEMENTS.

■ In the case of deep wet snow, you may even find it necessary to head straight down the fall line.

■ Deeper wet snow will also be easier to navigate through if you keep your weight on your rear foot and keep your board's nose up so the board is able to plane over the surface more easily.

■ Also, brush away any accumulated soggy snow that might be sticking to your board's deck. This will weigh you down significantly, and carrying such extra weight will make it almost impossible for you to plane over the deeper sections of snow.

■ Far from curtailing your form, analysing the run before starting it can be useful. Watch for deeper sections and steer away from them whenever possible. Go for steeper areas that will allow you to build up speed, and maximize this speed in preparation for upcoming flat sections.

Icy conditions
Whether it comprises overall bulletproof terrain resulting from a thaw and immediate freeze, or just a big blue patch in the middle of your favourite run, ice is the bane of all snowboarders. Compensate for the ice factor by remembering that a little movement goes a long way in this environment, and that there is usually a minimal margin (if any) for error.

■ When you encounter ice, keep your weight centred and your stance a little lower than usual. This will have the effect of maximizing your ability to keep your balance and will allow you to compensate very quickly if you begin to lose edge control.

■ In icy conditions, use very little upper body movement; turn using only your lower body and minimize your leaning and weight transferral.

■ Analyse the terrain ahead before you begin the run to avoid icy patches wherever possible. Alternatively, prepare to glide over them if they are unavoidable. Don't forget that the sideslip can be very useful in icy conditions; when the turn or traverse will not do the trick, a controlled sideslip over the treacherous area will be your salvation.

Tree riding technique

Start off slowly — look for tree-bound stretches along-side your favourite pistes and explore the fringes by popping in for a turn or two. This way you can begin to experiment without committing yourself to an entire run. If you like what you see and feel comfortable with the environment, probe a little further into the woods next time around.

When you feel confident that you are ready to explore an entire tree run, make sure you consult a map before charging in. You need to have a general idea of where you are, and where the run is likely to end up. If you don't, you could find yourself in a situation where you might have to hike for some time to get back to a lift-served area. Worse — and much more dangerously — you could end up getting lost. It is of vital importance just in case you ever do get lost or hurt to always ride with a buddy.

Never forget that tree riding involves risk. Wearing a helmet and goggles will protect your head and eyes in case of collision with unforeseen low-lying tree branches. Tree wells — left when the roots of downed trees are torn out of the ground — can be a major hazard. Falling into one of these hidden craters is a situation with a high potential for injury from which it can be difficult to extricate yourself. Always keep a sharp look-out for sources of danger and, when in doubt, err on the side of caution. Safety should always come first — you do not want your snowboarding experience cut short by avoidable accidents.

Riding steep terrain

Challenging yourself on steep terrain can be as exciting as snowboarding gets. For some riders, snowboarding offers no more exhilarating sensation than to conquer the fear that gripped them at the top of a treacherous-looking double-diamond run by successfully navigating their way down it.

Riding steeps simply exercises all of the skills you have acquired in order to make basic turns and edging manoeuvres. Do not, however, attempt to ride any steep run until you feel 100 per cent confident about your ability to do linked turns, stop, traverse and

IT'S EASY TO LOSE CONTROL ON STEEP TERRAIN — GET YOUR BOARD'S NOSE ACROSS THE FALL LINE QUICKLY.

sideslip on moderate terrain. Effective turning and confident stopping ability are crucial to your safety; traversing and sideslipping will be especially useful when you encounter advanced terrain.

Use the latter skills to navigate around obstacles such as icy patches, and to position yourself in the ideal location for your next turn. Also remember to pace yourself carefully when beginning to ride more advanced terrain. If you find yourself at the top of a run that looks too difficult for your level of ability, or one with conditions that are likely to spell danger, there is no shame in skipping it and saving it for another day. This way, you will ensure that there is another injury-free day on which to test your skills.

For your first attempt at riding steeps, choose a slope with good snow conditions that is relatively free of obstacles. Start off with the board across the fall line, your body in a crouched position with

RIDING 'FAKIE' (TAIL END FIRST) IS THE KEY TO LANDING AERIAL
SPIN TRICKS WITH CONFIDENCE.

knees bent and centre of gravity low. When you are ready to drop in and begin the run, hold this flexed-knee position when committing the first edge, straightening your upper body so that it is perpendicular to the angle of the slope. Remember that on steep runs, pointing the board straight down the fall line will launch you headlong into uncontrollably high speed, very quickly. When you begin your turn, point your head and upper body in the direction towards which you want to turn, then make sure to bring the board across the fall line and through the turn as quickly as possible. Once you have changed edges, stay low and bend your knees, using your legs as shock absorbers to compensate for any bumps or board chattering that may occur. Continue down the slope in this fashion, remembering to keep your position low and to use your sideslipping and traversing skills whenever necessary.

Freestyle

Freestyle riding is probably for many the most challenging and exciting aspect of the sport. Freestyle riders spend almost as much time in the air as they do on the snow, launching off 'hits' (man-made jumps of various types) in the terrain park and blasting off the walls of the halfpipe. Most people outside the snowboarding community believe that freestyle is the

sole domain of the young and the dare-devils. However, it is open to anyone — regardless of age or experience — as long as a safety-conscious approach is taken at first. Though many snowboarders may never become freestyle professionals that turn heads in the terrain park, knowledge of a few basic manoeuvres can ensure hours of fun.

Riding 'fakie'

Riding 'fakie' — with the tail end of the board forward — is a vital part of freestyle riding. Feeling comfortable with riding 'fakie' will come in very handy when you learn to perform more advanced tricks later on. Ideally, you should feel just about as relaxed about riding 'fakie' as you do riding forward. At least try to switch between the two stances and make a few 'fakie' turns if you want to have a go at freestyle riding. You should already be somewhat familiar with a basic 'fakie' traverse after mastering the 'falling leaf' (see pp 49-50). From there, practise regular traverses and then turning skills, just as you did to learn the basic riding movements. When learning to turn 'fakie', you might feel awkward at first due to the position of your rear (now your front) binding. Most freestyle riders make riding 'fakie' easier by opting for low stance angles, with both bindings straight across the board's width (see stance angle on p 24).

Once you have confidence in these skills, try to take at least one complete 'fakie' run each day. If you would rather break it up, switch your stance around whenever you come to a less-than-challenging stretch of terrain and practise there. This will help you to feel relaxed about switching your board direction mid-run, and will enhance your versatility.

The basic 'ollie'

Now that you've mastered all the basic movements on the snow, you are ready to take to the air. Derived from the skateboarding trick of the same name, the 'ollie' is snowboarding's most basic trick, and the main building block for learning more advanced tricks in the future. The 'ollie' lets you leave the ground without using a jump, by springing off the tail of the board. If taking up a skateboarding trick sounds intimidating at first, you will be pleased to know that the snowboarding version of the 'ollie' is actually much easier — for one thing, your feet stay attached to the board. And more importantly, if you do happen to fall, snow is a lot more forgiving than concrete.

Begin your first 'ollie' on a gentle, moderate slope with plenty of run-out space (see sequence below). Start heading down the fall line, board flat on the snow, in a centred stance position with your knees bent (A). When you are ready, shift your weight towards the tail by rocking backwards and lifting your front foot (B). This movement will flex the board, preparing you for takeoff. Just as the nose of the board comes off the snow, spring into the air by extending your rear leg. As the board snaps upward, pull up your rear leg, keeping the board level and staying in a crouched position (C). Stretch out your legs as you prepare to land, using your knees to absorb the shock of touching down (D). Try to land the tail end of the board first, and land flat on the board's base when

the rest of the board follows (E). When you feel the entire board on the snow, come to a complete stop.

Practise this manoeuvre until you feel you are able to perform a controlled, balanced 'ollie'. Then begin challenging yourself to go higher, faster. You may get quite daring, even attempting to challenge your abilities by 'ollieing' over obstacles, but make sure to pace yourself and always check out the landing area before attempting this. The 'air awareness' you gain from learning to 'ollie' will be the key to your future success when it comes to jumping.

The basic air or snowboard jump

Now that you are familiar with 'ollieing', you can take things up a notch with a basic air from a jump. The basic air utilizes very similar movements to the 'ollie'. However, it is not as pronounced. With the 'ollie', you create all of your own upward energy. When you are jumping, the jump itself provides much of the momentum and upward lift. The best place to start is the terrain park; head over there if your resort has

sequence ADAPTED FROM SKATEBOARDING, THE BASIC 'OLLIE' IS THE MOST FUNDAMENTAL TRICK IN SNOWBOARDING.

one. Man-made hits are all designed to help you catch air more easily. Start off with a small jump with a spacious landing area, and stay away from jumps with flat or over-used (dug-out) landings until you have the experience to cope with added difficulties. Keeping all this in mind, approach your first jump with plenty of

Rules of terrain park etiquette

■ Look before you leap. Always have a buddy check out the landing (or better yet, check it out for yourself). Often, you are not able to see the landing place from the approach. It will boost your confidence, and ensure your own safety, to know exactly what lies on the other side of the jump's lip.

■ Ask someone to stand at the side of the landing, to let others know you are coming down and to alert you when the landing area is clear.

■ Always check carefully that no one else is going at the same time as you. Many riders signal their approach by shouting 'dropping' as they take off — this warning is similiar to the golfers' 'fore'.

runway space between you and the jump. Head straight for the jump at a moderate speed with your board flat on the snow. Your body should be in a crouched position with your knees bent and your weight centred over the board. Stay in this position as you feel yourself gliding up the jump. When you approach the lip, launch yourself skyward by shifting your weight toward the tail and lifting your front foot. Like with the 'ollie', spring into the air when the nose of the board comes off the snow by extending your rear leg. Retract your rear leg as the board snaps upward, keep the board level and stay crouched and centred, balanced over your board. Remember to let the jump give you most of your momentum. Extend your legs as you prepare to land, and use your knees as shock absorbers to cushion the landing. Land flat on the board's base, with the tail end touching down first. When you feel the entire board on the snow, come to a complete stop.

As you grow in confidence, try taking off with a little more speed and launching higher and farther. When you feel relaxed about the basic air on a small jump, try it on some larger ones, but remember to pace yourself to your level of ability. As you feel yourself gaining more and more air awareness, try grabbing a rail in mid-air. This basic move adds stability in the air, and looks impressive.

Aerial spin tricks

Aerial spin tricks are a freestyle standard nowadays. Learning to launch and land from them takes a little work, but the learning process is fun and the feeling you get when you finally pull it off is justly rewarding.

In spin tricks, the most important difference between the 180 and the 360 is the incorporation of a lower-body twist. In the 180, you twist the upper body, and the lower body follows. To perform the 360 you

MANY PEOPLE NEVER REACH THE HEIGHTS THAT THIS BIG AIR COMPETITOR CAN, BUT IF YOU PACE YOURSELF AND FIND YOUR OWN COMFORT LEVEL YOU WILL STILL HAVE FUN.

sequence THE BASIC 180 IS THE FIRST SPINNING TRICK TO MASTER. STICK WITH THESE UNTIL YOU GAIN SOME 'AIR AWARENESS'.

have to actively twist your lower body once it begins to spin, adding the force that will bring the entire body full circle.

180 degree spin

The most basic spinning trick is the aerial 180 (see sequence above). As with the basic air (and this applies to any jump), check the jump and have someone check the landing to make sure the jump is clear of other riders before proceeding. Remember that before performing a spin, you should feel entirely confident about the controlled basic air, and be quite accomplished at riding 'fakie'.

Start off by approaching the jump at a controlled speed with a relaxed, bent-kneed stance and set the 'spring' by turning your upper body in the spinning direction (A). Hit the lip, spring off your edge and follow through the twist with your legs (B). Land 'fakie', with your head facing forward, legs extended and board level with the snow. Bend your knees as you land to absorb the impact (C).

Mastering the 180 degree spin will allow you to branch out with different variations of the same manoeuvre. It will also pave the way for learning the more advanced aerial 360. Continue to practise 180s until you gain confidence, then work on variations of the same trick. These include spinning in the opposite direction and approaching the jump 'fakie' and spinning around to land forward.

Aerial 360 spin

Learning to pull off a 360 aerial (see sequence overleaf) is a matter of building upon the skills you have honed while learning to launch and land a 180. The basic moves are identical — in essence, a 360 is just more of the same.

You will need extra speed to launch, in order to maximise on the height and distance travelled, you'll also have to push off and twist your upper body more energetically to make it all the way around.

Start by heading for the jump at a moderate speed, in a crouched position with your knees bent and your weight centred over your board. Instead of riding straight on the board's base as you did with the basic air, ride up the jump's transition on your toeside edge — you will need to push off strongly from the edge to initiate the spin (A). As you approach the lip, begin turning your head and shoulders in the direction you want to spin, for starters, turn them counter-clockwise. This upper-body motion will set the 'spring' that will force your lower body to follow in that direction and swing you into the spin once the board comes off the snow. As you hit the lip, spring upward off your edge (B) and continue to twist, allowing your lower body to complete the spin (C). As you feel your board swing around, turn your head to face forward and prepare to land the jump 'fakie' (D). Land with your legs extended and the board level over the snow (E), and cushion the landing by bending your knees (F).

A B C

D E F

sequence

YOU NEED SPEED, BALANCE AND PLENTY OF CONFIDENCE TO BEGIN
TRYING A 360 DEGREE SPIN, WHICH INVOLVES A FULL AERIAL ROTATION
WHILE GOING FORWARD. IT'S A GOOD IDEA TO FIRST PRACTISE A 360
SPIN ON FLAT GROUND WITHOUT YOUR SNOWBOARD BY JUMPING,
SPINNING AND LANDING.

Remember that no one, however athletic, is able to perform a 360 overnight. The air awareness and balance that is required can take some time to learn. Think of it as a process more than an end in itself, and work gradually towards spinning full circle. The important thing is to push your limits and to have fun, with due consideration for your own safety. If and when you do master this trick, persevere and keep up the challenge — your first 540 could be just over the horizon.

Halfpipe fundamentals

Riding the halfpipe has to be one of the most thrilling aspects of the freestyle experience, so it is no wonder that this particular type of snowboarding has grown exponentially in popularity over the last few years. Halfpipes seem to have sprung up everywhere overnight. Nearly every resort that welcomes snowboarders has its own professionally constructed and maintained halfpipe.

RESORTS WITH HALFPIPE FACILITIES OFTEN HOLD CONTESTS THAT HAVE GREAT SPECTATOR APPEAL AND PROVIDE AN IDEAL OPPORTUNITY TO LEARN FROM THE PROFESSIONALS.

Getting started in the halfpipe may seem like a daunting prospect for the new initiate. The best advice is to take a gradual approach to the halfpipe so that your first experiences will be not only exciting, but safe. Once you pluck up the courage to try, you will be surprised at how easy it is to master the basics.

For first-timers, looking down the barrel of the halfpipe from the top is nothing short of terrifying. To quell those initial fears, just take a run right down the middle of the pipe to familiarize yourself with the feeling of being inside one.

Once you have trekked back to the top of the half-pipe, the next step is to learn to ride the transitions (the sections of the half-pipe which form a link between the flat bottom and the vertical walls) for the frontside wall. For regular footers, this means the right-hand wall; for goofy-footers, the left.

■ You should be in a regular stance position with your knees bent and upper body straight, and your head and shoulders facing in the direction of travel.

■ When you come to the wall, bank a nice, easy turn off the transition — no need to go up the wall yet — just concentrate on performing the turn and absorbing the transition by bending your knees.

■ Once you have switched edges, head toward the rear wall. When you reach the backside transition,

bank another nice, easy turn, but this time riding on your heelside.

■ Again, concentrate on absorbing the transition with your knees. Continue on down the pipe, but stay on the transitions all the way down. Make several runs like this until you feel confident with this movement.

■ Next, practise making jump turns off the walls. As before, start on your toeside and head toward the frontside wall in a regular stance position at a moderate speed.

■ When you come to the wall, crouch down, bend your knees and continue up the transition and onto the wall. As you feel your momentum begin to slow, push off the wall, turn your head and torso in the direction of your turn and swing the board round, landing on the wall with your heelside edge.

■ Stay crouched and ride down the transition, absorbing it with your knees. Head for the backside wall, and make the heelside jump turn the same way, making sure to stay low and absorb the transition with your knees. As before, continue down the pipe making a series of toeside and heelside jump turns all the way down.

■ Continue to practise jump turns on the lower parts of the walls until you feel comfortable with them. Then begin to gradually push yourself higher up the walls by making your approach with greater speed.

■ Be careful not to push off too far once you begin to attain higher levels, or you will miss the wall and transition, and land on the flats — a move that will squander all of your momentum and could badly bruise both your body and your ego.

■ Remember to concentrate on maintaining your momentum by landing at a moderate downhill angle. Keep practising until eventually you'll be able to reach the top of the wall, and ultimately, turn in the air above the lip of the wall.

■ This will not happen overnight, so pace yourself, have fun and continue to push your limits in a safe, controlled manner.

■ Also, remember that straight frontside and backside turns in the pipe are just the beginning — try to incorporate 180s and 'fakie' riding into your style when you feel that you are ready.

■ You can learn a lot by watching other riders in the pipe, so keep your eyes open for ideas on tricks and tips on form.

Carving

For some snowboarders, carving is something to do on days when the conditions are ideal. For many others, precision carving is the only way to go. Laying out high-speed arcs on groomed corduroy is such a thrill that you may well try it and decide that your board never needs to leave the ground again. Learning to carve is really just a continuation and broadening of the skills you acquired when learning the basic turns.

Although you utilized the board's sidecut and flex when making basic turns, the board is actually almost skidding when it moves across the fall line. A skidded turn harnesses much of the board's energy and design, but also causes the board to slip sideways as it crosses the fall line. This creates the resistance that slows you down in order to control the movement. With a true carved turn, only the board's edge is used when making the turn — the rider never loses any forward momentum — and speed is controlled entirely through the arcing motion of the board.

A PRACTISE TOESIDE CARVING TURNS IF YOU'RE NEW TO AN ALPINE RACE/CARVING SET-UP.

B A HEELSIDE CARVING TURN IS FAR MORE RESPONSIVE WITH HARD BOOTS AND A HIGHER STANCE ANGLE.

Generally speaking, a hard-boot setup and alpine carving board are needed in order to achieve the control and response necessary for pure carving. If you are used to riding with a soft-boot setup, riding with an alpine board and hard boots will take some getting used to. The most noticeable difference will be a less forgiving feel due to the stiffness of the board and the rigid-shelled boots.

Also, you will be riding with a much higher binding angle to accommodate the narrowness of the alpine carving board (see stance angle, p 24). It would be a good idea to spend a few hours just getting used to riding with a carving setup before you begin working on your carving exercises.

When you feel ready to begin carving, find a moderate groomed slope with plenty of width and little or no fluctuation in contour. Start by linking carved traverses across the fall line. Your weight should be centred over the board, with your head and torso facing in the direction of travel and your arms at your sides, not leading and trailing. Turn as you normally do but concentrate on keeping the board entirely on its edge — this action will be facilitated by the respon-

COMPETITIVE SLALOM RACING CHALLENGES PARTICIPANTS TO MOVE THROUGH A SET COURSE IN THE FASTEST TIME

siveness of the hard-boot setup. Make sure your head and upper body continue to face in the direction of your turn. Most importantly, as you turn, try to eliminate any skidding. Make the tail of the board follow the exact path that the nose did when initiating the turn, using the same point for both entry and exit.

After completing a few turns this way, stop and analyze your tracks; the path should be a thin, arced line across the slope. If you cut a wide swathe when you turned, the board is still skidding. Continue practising these carved traverses until you can see from your tracks that you are utilizing only your edges on the turns. As you begin to feel confident about carving turns across the slope, try carving at greater

speeds and gradually work towards increasing your angle of descent so that you are heading more vertically down the fall line.

Also, start to work on creating shorter arced turns. You can accomplish this by bringing the board higher on the turning edge — the higher the edging angle, the sharper your turn will be. As you gain proficiency, you will be able to lay out your carves so that your upper body is horizontal to the snow. These so called 'Vitelli turns' are the height of style, and the true essence of high-speed carving.

Competitive snowboarding

For some intrepid riders, recreational riding is not enough — they enjoy testing their skills against those of rival snowboarders in organized competitions.

Although such competitions have been run for many years, the sport has only recently started to receive the acceptance and respect it deserves in this area. The most notable evidence of its respectability has been the acceptance of snowboarding as an official discipline of the Winter Olympics.

Though most snowboarders will never become Olympic competitors, there are plenty of opportunities to compete with their peers, within their own levels of skill and ability.

Racing

Snowboard racing is a competitive discipline that is popular with riders and spectators alike. Both racing and halfpipe riding are now official events in the Winter Olympics. The main forms of racing competition are Slalom, Giant Slalom, Super Giant Slalom (known as 'Super G') and Dual Slalom. Slalom events consist of two runs per rider down a racecourse with closely placed gates. The rider with the lowest average time after completing two runs, is the winner.

In Giant Slalom and Super G races, the format remains the same. However, the distances between the gates on the course is greater in the Giant and Super G races than in the regular slalom race course. Widely spaced gates mean that higher speeds are possible which requires more advanced levels of ability.

Dual Slalom events pit two racers against each other, in a head-to-head race to the finish line. If your local resort has a slalom course, there are likely to be specific times when it is available to anyone on the

HALFPIPES ARE BECOMING INCREASINGLY POPULAR AS THEY PROVIDE THE FORUM FOR RIDERS TO PERFECT DARING FREESTYLE TRICKS.

mountain. If you are keen to try a course, ask the resort for more information. Throughout the season, many resorts run open-entry events for which entrants pay a small fee. Check with your local resort about upcoming dates for these events, as well as those for amateur and professional spectator events.

Halfpipe competitions

As spectator sports these spectacular competitions are hard to beat. Competitors are judged on a series of runs in the pipe, which are assessed according to the difficulty of manoeuvres performed, as well as their successful execution. All resorts with their own halfpipes have made them generally accessible to everyone who would like to use the facility. So start your training there.

Check with your local resort whether they host open-entry competitions during the season (as a general rule the only requirement is an entry fee). Although official amateur and professional contests are limited to qualified competitors, it's worthwhile to attend as a spectator — you can learn a great deal from watching the professionals ride.

Boardercross

As the name implies, boardercross is a combination between motocross and snowboarding. Generally it consists of a six-person race on a downhill course kitted out with jumps, tunnel-like 'snake runs' and a variety of other obstacles. Boardercross is primarily a race against time while successfully completing an entire course. As participants are usually packed together in close contention, there is often a contact element involved, in the form of a collision or two. As a result, competitors wear helmets and protective pads and most of them compete in hard-boots setups, which allow for maximum speed and precision.

Getting started is as simple as locating a boardercross course at your local resort and trying it out. The resort's information service will give you details about how to enter the competitive field. In most cases, open-entry events (usually for a fee) are scheduled regularly during the course of the season.

BECAUSE BOARDERCROSS EVENTS INVOLVE SOME CONTACT AND
CHALLENGING OBSTACLE COURSES, HELMETS AND PADS ARE A MUST.

Amateur and professional competitions are of course open only to qualified competitors, but the thrills and spills of boardercross offer great spectator value. Consult the local information bureau to find out about forthcoming events.

Backcountry boarding

The increasing popularity of backcountry riding marks a return to the very roots of snowboarding. In the early days of the sport, when most resorts shunned board riders, they retreated to the backcountry areas in order to find places to ride.

Although today's snowboarders no longer have the problem of finding in-bounds riding, the main motivation behind going out into the backcountry is still the potent lure of unspoiled landscapes, pristine snow conditions and the precious solitude on a level that cannot be found in a commercial winter resort.

Backcountry safety

■ **Take an avalanche safety course or clinic.** These educational opportunities provide invaluable hands-on experience in personal safety and rescue techniques. (Excellent courses on basic and advanced avalanche skills are offered by organizations such as the National Ski Patrol of America and the Ski Club of Great Britain).

■ **Read up on avalanches.** Supplement what you've learned in the courses by obtaining as much additional information as you can. Always maintain a healthy respect for nature, no matter how experienced you are at backcountry skiing or snowboarding.

■ **Learn to recognize avalanche terrain.** Most avalanches travel in paths, on smooth exposed slopes of between 25 and 60 degrees, but there are many exceptions. To make an informed assessment of avalanche danger, it's essential to understand the significance of various terrain features, including slope angles, rocks, cornices and other wind-snow formations, ledges, and vegetation.

■ **Practise searching** for your companions' avalanche transceivers, a radio signalling device used to locate buried avalanche victims. Rehearse this until everyone you'll be travelling with feels confident about his or her ability to locate each beacon as quickly as possible. It takes only one incident to realize the importance of this level of preparation.

■ **Do your homework.** Always research your route and snow conditions in the exact location(s) you plan to snowboard or ski.

■ **Call your local avalanche warning centre** and check the current and forecasted weather before heading into the backcountry. Be prepared to adjust plans and/or routes accordingly.

■ **Remember and anticipate the 'Human Factor'.** Consider that people may exhibit undesirable behaviour in stressful situations. Your attitude and those of your companions can often mean the difference between a safe trip and catastrophe. Make sure you travel with people who have similar goals and attitudes.

Once you're in the backcountry

■ **Always carry avalanche equipment,** including avalanche transceivers, probes, and shovels (in addition to basic camping gear, extra clothing, high-energy food and plenty of water). Every member of the group needs to carry all three of these avalanche rescue items, and know how to use them.

■ **Be aware of your surroundings.** Stay alert, and constantly be on the lookout for information about the environment that indicates the potential for a slide. This includes recent avalanche activity and changes in terrain, snowpack and the weather.

■ **Analyze the snowpack stability.** As with studying terrain features, reading snowpack takes years of experience. There are, however, several tests that reveal the layers of a snow field and can help assess the risks involved with unstable snow. These include ski-pole tests, snowpit tests and resistance tests.

■ **Cross potential avalanche slopes one at a time.** If you doubt a slope's stability but still intend to cross it, only expose one person at a time to the potential danger. When climbing or traversing, each person should be at least 91m (100yd) from the next person. Travellers should climb steep narrow chutes one at a time, and when descending the slope, snowboard it alone. This not only minimizes the number of people who might get caught (and maximizes the number of people available for rescue), but reduces the stress put on the snowpack.

■ **Have the courage to know when you shouldn't go.** In the words of a Colorado expert in avalanche safety, 'No turns are worth putting friends and family through the ordeal of your death'.

(Guidelines reprinted with permission of the National Ski Patrol.)

The beauty of the backcountry experience is that it can be enjoyed as an afternoon ride accessed by a snowshoe hike, or as a full winter camping excursion that may last for several days. The best and most usual way to approach backcountry riding as a novice is with the assistance of an experienced guide. Guides can be

AVALANCHES OCCUR WITHOUT WARNING AND CAN BE DEADLY, SO NEVER GO BACKCOUNTRY RIDING WITHOUT BEING ADEQUATELY PREPARED.

hired through your local resort or via an advertised private service, based nearby. Spectacular areas of unconquered wilderness can provide some of the most breathtaking conditions and terrain accessible to riders but it is worth remembering that backcountry riding is associated with considerable risk.

In essence, there is no manual to teach you the multi-faceted skills you require to snowboard safely in wilderness areas. Taking an avalanche awareness course run by a specially qualified instructor is the only way to ensure that you know exactly how to avoid potentially life-threatening hazards, and how best to prevent avalanches from happening near you. In the worst-case scenario, the lessons will enable you to react appropriately in the event of one occurring.

The guidelines (pp 69-71) outline the basic rules of backcountry safety. They should be read carefully and put into practice. However, they are definitely not intended to replace a certified training course.

■ **Don't overlook clues.** Evidence of potential avalanche hazards will be there, so pay attention. If you educate yourself and always communicate with your companions, you should have the tools needed to make smart decisions when you are in the backcountry.

■ **Try to avoid travelling in the backcountry alone.** Also, never leave the group. Otherwise, if you run into trouble in the wilderness, you'll be on your own.

■ **Don't assume avalanches occur only in obvious large paths.** While most slides travel on broad, steep and smooth slopes, they can also wind down gullies or through forested areas. Remember if you can ski or snowboard through it, an avalanche can slide through it.

■ **Never travel in the backcountry** on the day after a big storm. Allow the snowpack to settle for at least 24 hours.

■ **Don't assume a slope is safe because there are tracks going across it.** Wind, sun, and temperature changes are constantly altering snowpack stability. What was safe yesterday (or this morning) could slide this afternoon. Furthermore, when you cross a slope you apply stress to the snowpack, which can cause it to slide.

■ **Don't assume there is no danger just because you're wearing a transceiver.** Although a transceiver is vital when travelling in remote areas, don't assume that it guarantees your safety.

■ **Don't allow your judgment to be clouded** by the desire to ride the steepest pitch or get the freshest snow. Staying alive should always be your main priority.

■ **Don't hesitate to voice concerns or fears.** As seasoned experts agree, 'No one is going to criticize you for wanting to be safe in the backcountry'.

■ **Don't consider yourself an avalanche expert.** Just because you've attended some courses and travelled extensively in the backcountry does not mean you know everything about avalanches.

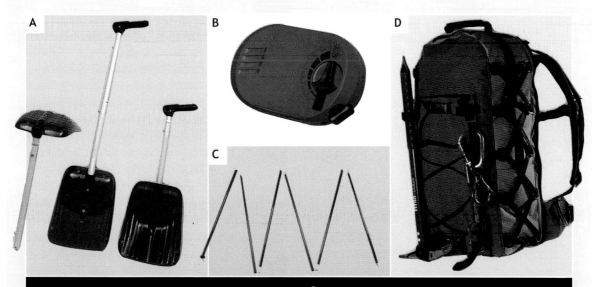

THE BASIC ESSENTIALS OF AVALANCHE EQUIPMENT

A AVALANCHE SHOVELS ARE USED TO DIG OUT AVALANCHE VICTIMS BUT CAN ALSO BE USED TO BUILD SNOW SHELTERS.

B AN AVALANCHE TRANSCEIVER TRANSMITS AND RECEIVES A CONSTANT RADIO SIGNAL TO LOCATE BURIED AVALANCHE VICTIMS.

C AVALANCHE PROBES ARE USED TO PINPOINT BURIED AVALANCHE VICTIMS ONCE THEY'VE BEEN LOCATED WITH A TRANSCEIVER.

D A BACKCOUNTRY DAYPACK IS USED TO CARRY FIRST AID ITEMS AND EQUIPMENT AND ENABLES YOU TO CARRY A BOARD ON YOUR BACK WHILE HIKING.

Safety and Precautions

as with any outdoor recreational activity, snowboarding has some potential risks that need to be recognized. Precise knowledge of the risks involved is the first step in preventing avoidable accidents and injuries. Generally speaking, the types of head and body injuries that snowboard riders are prone to are usually trivial in nature.

Protect yourself!

However, it makes sense to protect yourself from harm by wearing protective clothing and taking other commonsense steps to stay safe on the slopes. Not all injuries result from wipeouts (falls or spills). It's easy to strain a muscle, especially if you aren't conscientious about following a regular regimen of stretching exercises to keep your body supple, or if you fail to warm up adequately before you ride.

Safety does not begin and end with body preparation and the right padded clothing — it is very important to know how to conduct yourself on the mountain, or in the terrain park. This means understanding the potential environmental hazards connected with winter sports activities.

It is equally important to know how to read a resort's trail map. This ensures that you ride terrain designed to specially cater for your specific level of ability. Relative newcomers to snow sports should also spend some time familiarizing themselves with the rules of the resort. They need to learn how to ride responsibly and with due consideration for the safety of other snowboarders. True, snowboarding is all about having fun — but if you understand and recognize the potential risks you will be empowered to have much more fun, for longer. Spend some time reading about precautions, possible hazards and safety issues and you will be surprised how quickly riding safely and responsibly becomes second nature.

above IT MAKES SENSE TO WEAR A DECENT HELMET AND A PAIR OF GOGGLES, LIKE THIS YOUNG FREERIDER, TO MINIMIZE THE RISK OF INJURIES WHILE HAVING FUN.

opposite SAFETY IN SNOWBOARDING IS ALL ABOUT TAKING SENSIBLE PRECAUTIONS TO ENSURE YOU DON'T HAVE THE MISFORTUNE OF A WIPEOUT IN DEEP SNOW.

Safety Equipment

HELMETS ARE IMPORTANT PROTECTIVE
GEAR FOR BOTH BEGINNERS AND
ADVANCED RIDERS.

Prevent common injuries

■ Head and body injuries

As a newcomer to snowboarding, you have probably learned
the hard way about the 'beginner's body slam' — a term that
needs no further explanation.

■ Wipeouts like these can be a
bruising experience (to body
and ego) but the injuries
sustained are usually minor.
However, as the novice becomes
more confident and progresses
to levels of greater ability, the
possibility of real injury
increases dramatically.

■ To ensure an injury-free
experience both as a beginner
and advanced snowboarder, it is
wise to invest in protective
clothing that is specifically
designed for snowboarding.

■ **HELMETS** are used by
increasingly large numbers of
riders these days, especially
since more freestyle enthusiasts
are concentrating on 'going big'
and testing the limits in the
park and pipe. Freeriders who
take to the trees or enjoy riding
more extreme terrain can also
benefit from the safety of
sensible head protection.

■ These helmets (graphically
known as 'brain buckets') are
lightweight, comfortable and
don't obstruct your vision.

■ Made of strong plastic, helmets are 'breathable' in the
sense that the padding inside
'wicks' moisture away from the
head and releases excess heat
from holes in the plastic frame.

■ **WRIST GUARDS** can literally
make or break your first forays
into snowboarding. If and when
you fall forward (and you will),
your natural response is to
instinctively break your fall by

extending your hands out in
front of you to protect your
head and body.

■ Avoid falling on your hands as
it can cause an over-extension
of your wrists, which may result
in a nasty sprain; or worse. Each
wrist guard is equipped with a
brace to prevent overextension.

■ Most are lightweight and are
designed to fit easily under
your gloves or mittens.

■ **KNEE and BUTT PADS**
These cushion your knees and
buttocks, and are designed to
provide additional protection
to the two areas of your body
most likely to make contact
with the snow (or ice) in the
case of a wipeout.

■ These items are readily
available in most snowboarding
shops. Some shops even include
these protective pads (along
with wrist guards) in their
snowboard rental packages
for beginner riders.

Be prepared — bring a First Aid Kit

A compact and sturdy First Aid Kit to cater for basic emergencies should
be carried in your board bag. This is especially important
if you go snowboarding in the backcountry or remote
wilderness areas. Make sure that you include essentials
such as gauze swabs, cotton wool, waterproof
plasters, scissors, basic tablets (analgesic,
anti-diarrhoea and anti-histamine), eye
drops, antiseptic ointment and thermometer.

Prevent muscle strain

As with any vigorous physical activity, it is important to warm up before snowboarding, and also to warm down at the end of the day. A brief aerobic warm-up and stretching session will prevent muscle injury, increase flexibility and help you to ride significantly better than you would without warming up beforehand.

Ideally, you should have a proper series of stretching exercises to promote flexibility and suppleness. At the very least, stretch the main muscle groups before heading out for a day's riding.

Basic stretching exercises
Quadriceps stretch

Start by standing roughly an arm's length away from a chair or other suitable stabilizer (A). Stretch by bending your left leg, grabbing your foot by the ankle with your right hand and pulling the heel toward your buttocks (B). Stabilize yourself with the wall or chair if necessary. Pull gradually until you feel tension in the front of your thigh, then hold the position for 10 to 15 seconds. Repeat with the other leg (C) and continue to alternate until you have stretched each quadricep muscle three times.

Hamstring and lower back stretch

Sit on the floor with your left leg straight out in front of you, and the right one bent at a 90-degree angle (D) with the right foot against the inner thigh of the straightened leg — your legs should be in a 'figure-four' position. Start by gradually reaching down toward the foot of the straight leg with both hands (E). (You should feel the stretch in the back of your leg as well as the lower part of your back.) Hold this pose at a comfortable stretch for 10 to 15 seconds. Then, switch legs and repeat on the other side (F). Perform three stretches on each leg. Work gradually towards being able to hold your foot with your hands as you stretch.

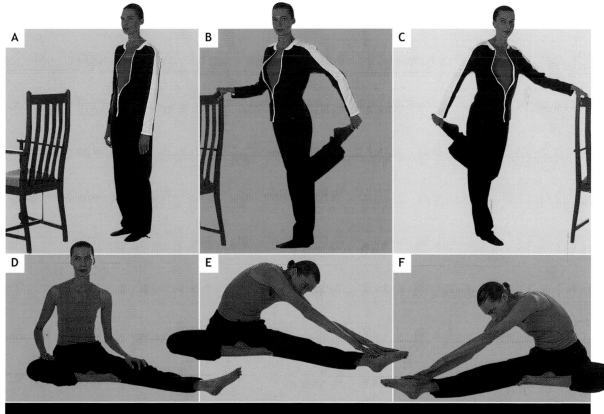

sequence STRETCHING EXERCISES FOR QUADRICEP (A,B AND C) AND HAMSTRING AND LOWER BACK MUSCLES (D,E AND F).

Calf stretch

Stand half an arm's length from a wall, facing the wall and with your legs in a scissor position. The left foot is slightly behind the right foot (A). Place hands against the wall at about head height, then bend the back knee gradually until you feel tension in your rear calf (B). Hold for 10 to 15 seconds. Switch positions, repeat with the other leg (C). Alternate until you've stretched each calf muscle three times.

Groin stretch

Sit on the floor with your legs bent, the knees facing outward and the soles of your feet together (D). Start by pulling your feet toward you until they are a few inches from your crotch, and then hold them there while you lean forward gradually (E). Do not jerk and keep the movement slow and controlled. Hold the position for 10 to 15 seconds or until you start to feel tension in the groin area.

sequence STRETCHING EXERCISES FOR CALVES (A, B AND C) AND GROIN MUSCLES (D AND E).

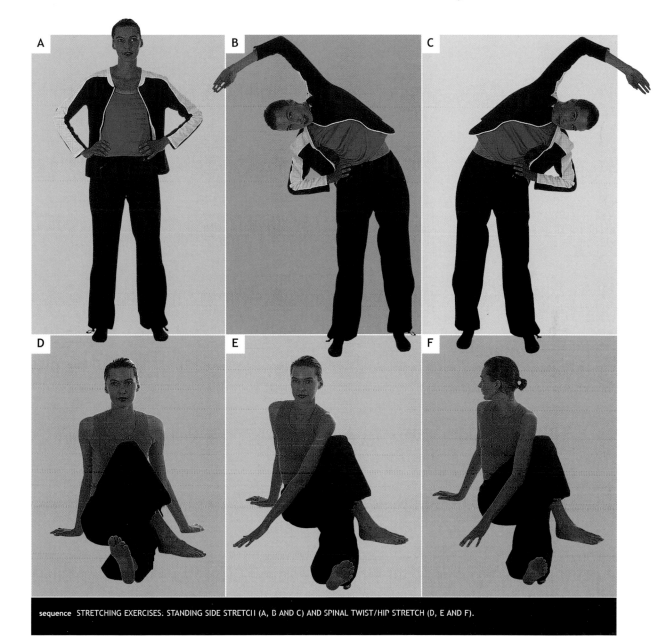

sequence STRETCHING EXERCISES. STANDING SIDE STRETCH (A, B AND C) AND SPINAL TWIST/HIP STRETCH (D, E AND F).

Standing side stretch

Stand with your feet roughly shoulders' width apart and your hands placed on your hips (A). Begin by lifting your right hand slowly up and over your head while leaning over your left side (B).

Make sure that you lean straight over sideways, and hold the position when you begin to feel a pulling sensation along the right side of your torso. Hold the position for 10 to 15 seconds, then repeat with the other side (C).

Spinal twist/hip stretch

Sit with your left leg straight out in front of you, your right leg bent and crossed over your left knee (D). Start by putting your left upper arm against the outside of your right knee and gently push the right knee inward while putting your right hand on the floor behind you (E). Twist your torso clockwise until you are looking over your right shoulder (F). Hold the position for 10 to 15 seconds or until you feel the tension along your hip and spine. Change sides and repeat exercise.

Insurance matters

Apart from any other precautions you may take to protect yourself from injury — such as having suitable clothing and equipment — having appropriate insurance is essential for any snowboarding holiday.

It goes without saying that common sense should prevail whenever you take part in a high-risk adventure sport like snowboarding: obey the 'rules of the road' on the mountain and in the terrain park and don't engage in activities that are beyond your level of ability and skill.

Tips on travel insurance

■ Travel insurance packages cover most contingencies, but it's important to shop around for an established and reputable company or insurance broker before taking out adventure insurance.

■ Check the small print to establish that the policy specifically includes snowboarding.

■ Adventure insurance packages should include costs of loss or damage to equipment, cover for delays, the costs of mountain search and rescue, evacuation and immediate medical treatment or hospitalization. Get legal advice if you are unsure.

■ Remember that your insurance could be invalidated if you deliberately ignore warnings of avalanche or other safety indicators posted in the resort, such as barriers closing off certain unsafe runs.

■ Check that your policy specifically covers you in certain conditions such as deep powder, the boardpark and in the pipe. If you are visiting a snowboarding resort, establish whether you are expected to sign a legal waiver or indemnity form before snowboarding.

■ In most cases, your lift ticket acts as a legal waiver for the resort — when you buy and use a lift pass, you are releasing the resort from any liability with regard to a personal injury that may occur while taking part in any activities on the premises.

■ 'Carte Neige', a worldwide organization that covers helicopter search and rescue missions only, is a useful top-up to your regular travel insurance policy which can often be bought with lift passes. However, don't view it as a suitable replacement for other insurance as it only covers you for on-mountain rescue and removal and subsequent limited medical treatment. Carte Neige also does not cover any form of snowboarding competition.

Environmental hazards

The thrill of snowboarding involves a certain degree of risk and it's best not to learn the hard way on a snow-covered mountain. Learning to anticipate and recognize the potential pitfalls of this environment is the first step to avoiding trouble. It is also the best way to ensure that all your time is spent having fun.

Dehydration

This occurs when the body loses an excessive amount of fluid. People who are not acclimatized to high altitude and dry mountain air are especially vulnerable to dehydration. Watch out for symptoms such as excessive thirst, loss of appetite, headache, nausea and dizziness. Avoid dehydration by ensuring you have a continual intake of water before, during and after your day on the slopes. Also, stay away from drinks containing caffeine. This substance acts as a diuretic and will actually accelerate dehydration.

Remember that the symptoms lag behind the condition, so don't wait until you feel thirsty to start drinking water. A good rule of thumb is to drink at least 200—400ml (one-third to two-thirds of a pint) of water for every 20 minutes of exercise.

Hypothermia

Hypothermia is defined as a potentially serious condition in which the overall body temperature drops well below normal. The drop in body heat results from exposure to low temperatures, and occurs especially after the body's energy supplies have been exhausted. The most common symptoms of mild hypothermia are withdrawal and shivering, although more serious hypothermia can cause confusion and collapse. Prevention is better than cure – dress sensibly for the weather conditions and ensure a reasonably steady intake of carbohydrates to maintain normal blood sugar levels.

If you suspect that you – or someone with you – is becoming hypothermic, seek warmth and shelter immediately. Warm up with drinks such as hot chocolate and extra clothing or blankets. Avoid tea, coffee or alcholic drinks as they may depress or stimulate the nervous system. If the victim's condition appears to be deteriorating, get him or her to a First Aid Station or hospital as soon as possible.

Altitude

High mountain air is far less saturated with oxygen than that found closer to sea level. The average person usually takes about two to three days to become acclimatized to the thinner air found at high altitudes.

If you are not fully acclimatized, the most obvious symptom will be an apparent loss of aerobic ability. This means that any activity that you would normally be able to carry out with ease, will probably leave you breathless in the beginning.

Remember to take it slowly: pace yourself and accept that you will get fatigued much more quickly than usual. High altitude also tends to heighten the effects of alcohol consumption; so steer clear of any alcohol when you are out riding.

Frostbite

This dangerous condition results from exposure to intense cold and can cause severe tissue damage. It commonly first appears in body extremities such as the fingers and toes,

EXERCISE CAUTION BY APPLYING SUNTAN LOTION WITH AN SPF FACTOR OF 15 OR HIGHER.

or in exposed areas like the face, especially the nose. If you are planning to ride in extremely cold conditions, make sure you do not leave any areas of the body exposed by wearing proper protective clothing. Be vigilant and go indoors at the first sign of numbness or loss of sensation. If you think that you or a snowboarding companion may have been overexposed, seek medical attention.

Ultraviolet radiation (sunburn)

People tend to underestimate the amount of ultraviolet (UV) radiation found in snow and mountain conditions and are often unaware of the dangers. Wearing a hat to block the sun is simply not enough to protect yourself from harmful UVA and UVB rays. Snow reflects up to 80 per cent of the sun's rays. (UVA and UVB rays cause sunburn and tanning, while UVB rays causes skin ageing and wrinkling). As with watersports such as sailing or windsurfing, most UV radiation can come from below. UV rays reflected off the snow's surface are just as powerful as those coming from the sky above, even when it is cloudy, misty or overcast.

Tips to avoid sunburn
■ Always cover any exposed areas liberally with a water-resistant, broad-spectrum sunscreen that protects against both UVA and UVB rays.
■ Apply sunscreen at least 30 minutes before exposure so the lotion can penetrate the skin's upper layer.
■ The cream should have a Sun Protection Factor (SPF) of at least 15 or higher; anything below that is not an effective protective barrier.
■ The glare from UV rays can also be damaging to the eyes; never ride without goggles or a good pair of sunglasses that offer adequate UV protection.

Responsible riding

Most snowboarders would be delighted to have the slopes all to themselves; unfortunately, this is not often the case. An essential element of snowboarding safety is the ability to take the comfort and safety of others into consideration. As newcomers to the resort world, snowboarders have been criticized for being irresponsible and discourteous to fellow slope users. Know the rules and follow them. That way, you can help to dispel this undeserved stereotype.

Trail maps are important

Resorts go to great lengths to create up-to-date, user-friendly trail maps that provide details of all the terrain open to you. Trail maps are distributed freely and are readily available — you can always find one at the booth where you buy your lift ticket, in the lodge or in the lift queue. Trail maps offer valuable information on locating first aid stations and also indicate the difficulty levels and steepness of slopes at a resort. It is important to consult a trail map whenever you ride and always keep a copy with you. That way, you can plan your routes, and stay away from trails that are too advanced for your level of ability. An added advantage of trail maps is that they help you identify a less crowded area that is suitable for you to experiment and gain more riding experience.

Riders prefer to focus on the fun aspect of snowboarding, but it is necessary to know where mid-mountain lodge areas and First Aid Stations are located in case there is an accident or you get into trouble. Consulting a trail map will maximize your riding time in the long run, by helping you find just the kind of runs you are looking for.

How to read a trail map

To help you plan a safe, enjoyable day's riding, all runs on the local trail map are marked according to their individual levels of difficulty. The difficulty marking is determined by expert observation of the steepness of the run and the overall difficulty of the terrain.

Although the symbols used to denote different types of terrain differ in North America from those used in resorts in Europe and elsewhere, the symbols will be clearly linked to an explanatory key on the trail map of each specific resort. If you are unsure, get professional advice from local resort staff.

It is important to recognize your own limitations and to stay within areas that offer the types of terrain which best suit your abilities. Even if you are an experienced snowboarder, don't let fellow riders persuade you to go treeriding or perform jumps off a cliff unless you are confident that you would be in full control. It's also worth remembering that the difficulty ratings on a trail map are always relative to the terrain at each resort. An intermediate run at a larger, more difficult mountain resort that is more suitable for expert riders may feel like an advanced run if you are used to riding at a smaller resort.

Your responsibility code

Snowboarding can be enjoyed in many ways. Regardless of how you decide to enjoy the slopes, always show courtesy to others and be aware that there are elements of risk in skiing and riding that common sense and personal awareness can help to reduce. Know the code. It's your responsibility.

■ Always stay in control, and be able to stop or avoid other people or objects.
■ People ahead of you have the right of way. It is your responsibility to avoid them.
■ You must not stop where you obstruct a trail, or are not visible from above.
■ Whenever starting downhill or merging into a trail, look uphill and yield to others.
■ Always make use of devices which help to prevent runaway equipment.
■ Observe all posted signs and warnings. Keep off closed trails and out of closed areas.
■ Prior to using any lift, you must have the knowledge and ability to load, ride and unload safely.

(Extract reprinted with permission of the National Ski Patrol).

NOTE THAT DIFFERENT STANDARDS AND DIFFICULTY LEVELS APPLY TO EUROPE AND NORTH AMERICA.

■ BEGINNER RUNS are marked with a green line (A) throughout Europe, and a green circle (B) throughout North America.

■ EASY RUNS are marked with a blue line (D) in Europe, while in North America a blue square (C) denotes intermediate terrain.

■ INTERMEDIATE terrain throughout Europe is marked with a red line (G).

■ DIFFICULT terrain is marked with a black line (H) in both Europe and North America.

■ North American resorts break down advanced terrain further by using a black diamond (E) to mark MORE DIFFICULT terrain, and a double black diamond (F) as the symbol for VERY DIFFICULT terrain.

■ OFF-PISTE routes in both Europe and North America are marked with a straight dotted line (I). While the trail is technically within the bounds of the resort, it is not regularly patrolled or groomed, and should only be ridden by those with expert skills and knowledge of backcountry safety. Consult a guide before visiting these areas.

■ LIFT TYPES are usually clearly marked with symbols for gondolas, chair lifts and drag lifts (pomas and t-bars). These can vary between resorts, but the symbol in use will be clearly marked in your map's key.

■ OTHER SYMBOLS include mid-mountain lodges, information areas and First Aid and Ski Patrol stations. These areas will be clearly marked on your resort's trail map and provide important guidelines.

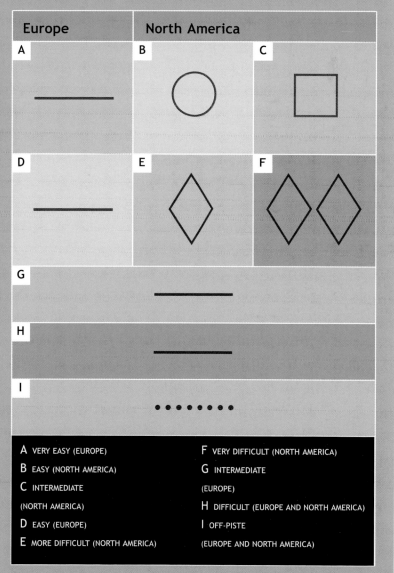

Europe	North America	
A	B	C
D	E	F
G		
H		
I		

A VERY EASY (EUROPE)
B EASY (NORTH AMERICA)
C INTERMEDIATE (NORTH AMERICA)
D EASY (EUROPE)
E MORE DIFFICULT (NORTH AMERICA)
F VERY DIFFICULT (NORTH AMERICA)
G INTERMEDIATE (EUROPE)
H DIFFICULT (EUROPE AND NORTH AMERICA)
I OFF-PISTE (EUROPE AND NORTH AMERICA)

Top Venues Worldwide

now that you're hooked, you need to choose a resort to enjoy your newfound skills. If you're a beginner, look for a snowboard-friendly resort that offers varying terrain, professional instructors and affordable rental equipment.

Major snowboarding organizations also offer valuable advice on good training schools and associations affiliated to the Fédération Internationale de Ski (FIS).

Training Schools

HIGH CASCADE SNOWBOARD CAMP
- PO BOX 368, Government Camp, OR 97028, USA
- Tel: +1 800 334-4272 or +1 541 389-7404
- E-mail: highcascade@highcascade.com
- Website: www.highcascade.com

SNOWBOARD CAMP OF CHAMPIONS
- Whistler, British Columbia, CANADA
- Tel: +1 604 938-3450
- E-mail: info@campofchampions.com
- Website: www.campofchampions.com

SKI CLUB OF GREAT BRITAIN
- 57-63 Church Road, London, SW19 5SB, UK
- Tel: +44 20 8410-2000
- Fax: +44 20 8410-2001
- Provides information on all wintersports
- Website: www.skiclub.co.uk

Snowboarding Associations

INTERNATIONAL
- Fédération Internationale de Ski (FIS)
- Switzerland
- Website: www.fis-ski.com

USA
- United States Ski and Snowboard Association
- Box 100, 1500 Kearns Blvd, Park City, UT 84060
- Tel: +1 435 649-9090
- Fax: +1 435 649-3613
- Website: www.ussa.org/snowboard/snowboard.htm

- United States of America Snowboard Association (USASA)
- PO Box 15500, South Lake Tahoe, CA 96151
- Website: www.usasa.org

CANADA
- Canadian Ski and Snowboard Association
- Suite 202, 1451 West Broadway
- Vancouver, BC V6H 1H6
- Tel: +1 604 734-6800
- Fax: +1 604 669-7954
- E-mail: canadaskiandsnowboard.net

UNITED KINGDOM
- British Ski and Snowboard Federation
- Snowsport GB, Hillend, Biggar Road
- Midlothian, EH10 7EF
- Tel: +44 131 445-7676
- Website: www.snowsportgb.com

opposite NEW ZEALAND'S TREBLE CONE RESORT BOASTS GREAT TERRAIN AND BREATHTAKING VIEWS OF LAKE WANAKA.

All resorts listed have ample beginner and intermediate terrain, and offer lessons and rental facilities as well as contact information to help you plan your trip.

CANADA

ALBERTA

- **LAKE LOUISE**
- 1 Whitehorn Road
- Lake Louise, Alberta, T0L 0C0
- Tel: +1 403 522-3555
- E-mail: info@skilouise.com
- Website: www.skilouise.com

- **BANFF/MT NORQUAY**
- Norquay Road
- Banff, Alberta, T0L 0L0
- Tel: +1 403 762-4421
- E-mail: admin@banffnorquay.com
- Website: www.banffnorquay.com

- **MARMOT BASIN**
- Highway 33
- Jasper National Park, Alberta, T0E 1E0
- Tel: +1 403 852-3816
- E-mail: info@skimarmot.com
- Website: www.skimarmot.com

- **SUNSHINE VILLAGE**
- Sunshine Access Road
- Banff, Alberta, T0L 0C0
- Tel: +1 403 760-5200
- E-mail: reservations@skibanff.com
- Website: www.skibanff.com

- **NAKISKA**
- PO Box 1988
- Kananaskis Village, Alberta, T0L 2H0
- Tel: +1 403 591-7777
- E-mail: info@skinakiska.com
- Website: www.skinakiska.com

BRITISH COLUMBIA

- **BIG WHITE**
- PO Box 2039, Station 'R'
- Kelowna, British Columbia, V1X 4K5
- Tel: +1 250 765-3101
- E-mail: mail@bigwhite.com
- Website: www.bigwhite.com

FERNIE IS KNOWN TO LOCALS OF BRITISH COLUMBIA, CANADA, AS A HAVEN FOR PRISTINE POWDER.

- **FERNIE**
- Ski Area Road
- Fernie, British Columbia, V0B 1M1
- Tel: +1 250 423-3515
- Website: www.skifernie.com

MOUNT WASHINGTON
- Courtenay, British Columbia, V9N 5N3
- Tel: +1 250 338-1386
- E-mail: ski@mtwashington.bc.ca
- Website: www.mtwashington.bc.ca

- **PANORAMA RESORT**
- Panorama, British Columbia, V0A 1T0
- Tel: +1 250 342-6941
- E-mail: paninfo@panoramaresort.com
- Website: www.panoramaresort.com

- **SILVER STAR**
- British Columbia, VIB 3MI
- Tel: +1 250 542-0224
- E-mail: reserv@junction.net
- Website: www.silverstarmtn.com

- **SUN PEAKS**
- 3150 Creekside Way St 50
- Sun Peaks, British Columbia, V0E 1Z1
- E-mail: info@sunpeaksresort.com
- Website: www.sunpeaksresort.com

- **WHISTLER/BLACKCOMB**
- 4545 Blackcomb Way, Whistler
- British Columbia, VON 1B4
- Tel: +1 604 938-3450 ■ E-mail: bscguestrelations@intrawest.ca
- Website: www.whistler-blackcomb.com

- **WHITEWATER**
- PO Box 60, Nelson
- British Columbia, V1L 5P7
- Tel: +1 250 354-4944
- E-mail: info@skiwhitewater.com
- Website: www.skiwhitewater.com

ONTARIO
- **CALABOGIE**
- Black Mountain Road
- Calabogie, Ontario, K0J 1H0
- Tel: +1 613 752-2720
- E-mail: peaks@calabogie.com
- Website: www.calabogie.com

- **MT ANTOINE**
- Highwy 533
- Mattawa, Ontario, P1B 8K1
- Tel: +1 705 474-9950
- E-mail: mantoine@onlink.net
- Website: www.onlink.net/mtantoine

QUEBEC
- **GRAY ROCKS**
- 525 Principal Road
- Mt Tremblant, Quebec, J0T 120
- Tel: +1 819 425-2771
- E-mail: info@grayrocks.com
- Website: www.grayrocks.com

- **MONT BLANC/FAUSTIN**
- 1006 Route 117
- St Fauschin, Quebec, J0T 2G0
- Tel: +1 819 688-2444
- E-mail: lcroteau@ski-mont-blanc.com
- Website: www.ski-mont-blanc.com

- **MONT STE ANNE**
- 2000 Beaupre Blvd
- Beaupre, Quebec, G0A 1E0
- Tel: +1 418 827-4561
- E-mail: info@mont-saint-anne.com
- Website: www.mont-sainte-anne.com

- **MONT SUTTON**
- 671 Maple
- Sutton, Quebec, J0E 2K0
- Tel: +1 514 538-2339
- E-mail: sutton@mt-sutton.com
- Website: www.mt-sutton.com

MONT CASCADE
- 448 Mont Cascade Road
- Cantley, Quebec, J8V 3B2
- Tel: +1 819 827-0301
- E-mail: cascades@istar.ca
- Website: www.montcascades.ca

- **TREMBLANT**
- 3005 Pineford Road
- Mont Tremblant, Quebec, J0T 1Z0
- Tel: +1 819 681-2000
- E-mail: info@tremblant.com
- Website: www.tremblant.com

USA

ALASKA

ALYESKA
- 1000 Arlberg Ave
- Girdwood, Alaska, 99587
- Tel: +1 907 754-1111
- E-mail: info@alyeskaresort.com
- Website: www.alyeskaresort.com

CALIFORNIA

BIG BEAR MOUNTAIN RESORT
- PO Box 5038
- Bear Valley, CA 95223
- Tel: +1 209 753-2301
- E-mail: bearmtn@boothcreek.com
- Website: www.bearmtn.com

BEAR VALLEY SKI AREA
- PO Box 5038
- Bear Valley, CA 95223
- Tel: +1 209 753-2301
- E-mail: ski@bearvalley.com
- Website: www.bearvalley.com

BOREAL MOUNTAIN PLAYGROUND
- PO Box 39
- Truckee, CA 96160
- Tel: +1 530 426-3666
- E-mail: info@borealski.com
- Website: www.borealski.com

HEAVENLY SKI RESORT
- PO Box 2180
- Stateline, NV 89449
- Tel: +1 800 243-2836 or +1 775 586-7000
- E-mail: info@skiheavenly.com
- Website: www.skiheavenly.com

JUNE MOUNTAIN SKI AREA
- PO Box 146
- June Lake, CA 95329
- Tel: +1 760 648-7733
- E-mail: aross@mammoth-mtn.com
- Website: www.junemountain.com

KIRKWOOD
- Lake Tahoe, CA
- Tel: +1 800 967-5808
- E-mail: kwd-info@ski-kirkwood.com
- Website: www.ski-kirkwood.com

MAMMOTH MOUNTAIN SKI AREA
- PO Box 24
- Mammoth Lakes, CA 93546
- Tel: +1 760 934-0745
- E-mail: 800mammoth@mammoth-mtn.com
- Website: www.mammothmountain.com

THE NEW MOUNTAIN HIGH RESORT
- 24510 Highway 2, Wrightwood, CA
- Tel: +1 760 246-5808
- E-mail: jcmmthigh@qnet.com
- Website: www.mthigh.com

NORTHSTAR AT TAHOE
- PO Box 129, Truckee, CA 96160
- Tel: +1 530 562-1010
- E-mail: northstar@boothcreek.com
- Website: www.skinorthstar.com

SIERRA AT TAHOE
- 1111 Sierra-At-Tahoe Road
- Twin Bridges, CA 95735
- Tel: +1 530 659-7453
- E-mail: sierra@boothcreek.com
- Website: www.sierratahoe.com

SNOW SUMMIT MOUNTAIN RESORT
- 880 Summit Blvd
- Big Bear Lake, CA 92315
- Tel: +1 909 866-5766
- E-mail: info@snowsummit.com
- Website: www.snowsummit.com

SNOW VALLEY MOUNTAIN SKI RESORT
- PO Box 2337
- Running Springs, CA 92382
- Tel: +1 909 867-2751 or +1 800 680-7669
- E-mail: info@snow-valley.com
- Website: www.snow-valley.com

SQUAW VALLEY, USA
- PO Box 2007
- Olympic Valley CA 96146
- Tel: +1 530 583-6955
- E-mail: squaw@squaw.net
- Website: www.squaw.com

COLORADO

ARAPAHOE BASIN
- Dillon County, CO
- Tel: +1 970 468-0718 or +1 888 272-7246
- E-mail: abasin@colorado.net
- Website: www.arapahoebasin.com

EXPANSIVE TERRAIN FOR ALL ABILITY LEVELS AND RELIABLE ROCKY MOUNTAIN POWDER SNOW MAKE VAIL THE PREMIER RESORT IN THE USA.

- **BUTTERMILK MOUNTAIN**
- PO Box 1248
- Aspen, CO 81612
- Tel: +1 970 925-1220
- E-mail: ewbaker@skiaspen.com
- Website:
www.skiaspen.com/mntinfo/
mnt_info_mnt_buttermilk.html

- **SNOWMASS**
- PO Box 1248
- Aspen, CO 81612
- Tel: +1 970 925-1220
- Website: www.skiaspen.com

- **BRECKENRIDGE SKI RESORT**
- Breckenridge, CO
- Tel: +1 970 453-5000 or
+1 800-789-SNOW (Tollfree)
- Website: www.breckenridge.com

- **COPPER MOUNTAIN**
- Dillon County, CO
- Tel: +1 800 458-8386
- E-mail: wc@ski-copper.com
- Website: www.ski-copper.com

- **PURGATORY AT DURANGO MOUNTAIN RESORT**
- 1 Skier Place, Durango, CO 81301
- Tel: +1 800-982-6103
- E-mail:
info@durangomountain.com
- Website: www.ski-purg.com

- **STEAMBOAT SKI & RESORT**
- 2305 Mt Werner Circle CO 80487
- Tel: +1 970 879-0740
- E-mail:
steamboat-info@steamboat-ski.com
- Website: www.steamboat-ski.com

- **TELLURIDE SKI & GOLF COMPANY**
- PO Box 11155
- Telluride, CO 81435
- Tel: +1 970 728-7485
- E-mail: jackiek@telski.com
- Website: www.telski.com

- **VAIL RESORTS**
- PO Box 7, Vail, CO 81658
- Tel: +1 970 476-4888
- E-mail: vailinfo@vailresorts.com
- Website: www.vail.com

MAINE
- **SUGARLOAF USA**
- Route 27
- Carrabassett Valley, Maine, 04947
- Tel: +1 207 237-2000
- E-mail: info@sugarloaf.com
- Website: www.sugarloaf.com

MONTANA

- **WHITEFISH MOUNTAIN RESORT**
- PO Box 1400
- Whitefish, MT 59937
- Tel: +1 406 862-2900
- E-mail:
info@skiwhitefish.com
- Website: www.skiwhitefish.com

- **BIG SKY SKI & SUMMER RESORT**
- 1 Lone Mountain Trail
- Big Sky, MT 59716
- Tel: +1 800 548-4486
- E-mail:
groupsales@bigskyresort.com
- Website: www.bigskyresort.com

NEW MEXICO

- **SKI SANTA FE**
- 2209 Brothers Road
- Suite 220, Santa Fe, NM 87505
- Tel: +1 505 982-4429
- E-mail: info@skisantafe.com
- Website: www.skisantafe.com

OREGON

- **MOUNT HOOD MEADOWS
SKI RESORT**
- Highway 35
- Mount Hood, Parkdale, OR 97041
- Tel: +1 503 227-SNOW
- Website: www.skihood.com

- **MT BACHELOR**
- 335 SW Century Drive
- Bend, OR 97702
- Tel: +1 541 382-2442
- Website: www.mtbachelor.com

UTAH

- **THE CANYONS**
- 4000 The Canyons Resort Drive
- Park City, UT 84098
- Tel: +1 435 615-8040
- E-mail: info@thecanyons.com
- Website: www.thecanyons.com

- **PARK CITY MOUNTAIN RESORT**
- 1310 Lowell Avenue
- Park City, UT 84098
- Tel: +1 435 649-8111
- E-mail: info@pcski.com
- Website:
www.parkcitymountain.com

- **SNOWBIRD**
- Highway 210, Little Cottonwood
- Canyon, Snowbird, UT 84092
- Tel: +1 801 742-2222
- E-mail: info@snowbird.com
- Website: www.snowbird.com

VERMONT

- **KILLINGTON RESORT & PICO
MOUNTAIN**
- 4763 Killington Road
- Killington, VT 05751
- Tel: +1 802 422-6200
- E-mail: info@killington.com
- Website: www.killington.com

- **MOUNT SNOW RESORT**
- 39 Mount Snow Road
- West Dover, VT 05356
- Tel: +1 802 464-3333
- E-mail: info@mountsnow.com
- Website: www.mountsnow.com

- **STOWE MOUNTAIN RESORT**
- 5781 Mountain Road
- Stowe, VT 05672
- Tel: +1 802 253-3000
- Website: www.stowe.com

- **STRATTON MOUNTAIN**
- RR #1, Box 145
- Stratton Mountain, VT 05155
- Tel: +1 802 297-2200
- E-mail:
mfuster@intrawest.com
- Website: www.stratton.com

WASHINGTON

- **MT BAKER**
- 1019 Iowa Street, Bellingham
- Washington, 98225
- Tel: +1 360 734-6771
- Website:
www.mtbakerskiarea.com

WYOMING

- **JACKSON HOLE
MOUNTAIN RESORT**
- PO Box 290
- Teton Village, WY 83025
- Tel: +1 307 733-2292
- E-mail: info@jacksonhole.com
- Website: www.jacksonhole.com

- **GRAND TARGHEE SKI &
SUMMER RESORT**
- Ski Hill Road
- PO Box SKI Alta, WY 83422
- Tel: +1 307 353-2300
- E-mail: info@grandtarghee.com
- Website: www.grandtarghee.com

EUROPE

ANDORRA

- **ARINSAL**
- Andorra ■ La Massana Province
- Tel: +376 83-8438
- Website: www.arinsal-andorra.com

- **GRAU ROIG/PAS DE LA CASA**
- Andorra ■ Encamp Province
- Tel: +376 80-1060
- Website: www.pasgrau.com

AUSTRIA

- **OBERTAUERN**
- Salzburg ■ Austria
- Tel: +43 6456 7252
- Website: www.obertauern.at

- **SCHLADMING**
- Styria ■ Austria
- Tel: +43 3687 22-268
- E-mail: stadtamt@schladming.at
- Website: www.schladming.co.at

- **INNSBRUCK**
- Tyrol ■ Austria
- Tel: +43 512 59-850
- E-mail: info2@innsbruck.tvb.co.at
- Website: www.innsbruck.info

- **ISCHGL**
- Tyrol ■ Austria
- Tel: +43 5444 52-660
- Website: www.ischgl.co.at
- **KIRCHBERG**

- Tyrol
- Austria
- Tel: +43 5357 2309
- Website: www.kirchberg.at

- **KITZBÜHEL**
- Tyrol
- Austria
- Tel: +43 5356 62-1550
- Website: www.skiaustria.com/kitzbuel/kitzbuel.htm

OBERTAUERN'S REPUTATION FOR GUARANTEED SNOW MAKES IT ONE OF THE MOST POPULAR DESTINATIONS IN AUSTRIA.

- **SOLDEN**
- 6450 Solden ■ Austria
- Tel: +43 57200 200
- E-mail: info@soelden.com
- Website: www.soelden.com

- **ST ANTON**
- Tyrol ■ Austria
- Phone: +43 5446 22-690
- Website:
www.stantonamarlberg.com

- **ST JOHANN**
- Tyrol
- Austria
- Tel: +43 5352 63-335
- Website: www.st.johannerhof.at

FRANCE
- **CHÂTEL**
- Alpes Du Nord ■ France
- Tel: +33 450 73-2244
- E-mail: touristoffice@chatel.com
- Website: www.chatel.com

- **AVORIAZ**
- Haute Savoie ■ France
- Tel: +33 450 74-0211
- E-mail:
avoriaz.ot@portesdusoleil.com
- Website: www.avoriaz.com

- **CHAMONIX/MONT BLANC**
- Haute Savoie ■ France
- Tel: +33 450 530-0024
- Website: www.chamonix.com

CHAMONIX HAS MANY GUIDE SERVICES TO GET
YOU TO ITS POTENTIAL OFF-PISTE AREAS.

- **MEGÈVE**
- Haute Savoie
- France
- Tel: +33 450 21-2728
- E-mail: megeve@megeve.com
- Website: www.megeve.com

- **MORZINE**
- Haute Savoie
- France
- Tel: +33 450 74-7272
- E-mail:
touristoffice@morzine-avoriaz.com
- Website:
www.morzine-avoriaz.com

- **LES DEUX ALPES**
- Isère
- France
- Tel: +33 476 79-2200
- Website: www.les2alpes.com

- **COURCHEVEL**
- Savoie
- France
- Tel: +33 479 80-029
- E-mail: pro@courchevel.com
- Website: www.courchevel.com

- **LA PLAGNE**
- Savoie
- France
- Tel: +33 479 97-979
- Website: www.la-plagne.com

- **MÉRIBEL**
- Savoie ■ France
- Tel: +33 479 86-001
- E-mail: info@meribel.net
- Website: www.meribel.net

- **LES ARCS**
- Savoie
- France
- Tel: +33 479 07-1257
- E-mail: lesarcs@lesarcs.com
- Website: www.lesarcs.com

- **TIGNES**
- Savoie
- France
- Tel: +33 479 40-0440
- E-mail: information@tignes.net
- Website: www.tignes.net

- **VAL D'ISERE**
- Savoie
- France
- Tel: +33 479 60-660
- E-mail: info@valdisere.com
- Website: www.valdisere.com

- **VAL THORENS**
- Savoie
- France
- Tel: +33 479 00-808
- Website: www.val-thorens.com

ITALY

- **CORTINA**
- Belluno
- Italy
- Tel: +39 0436 3231
- Website: www.sunrise.it/cortina

- **LIVIGNO**
- Sondrio
- Italy
- Tel: +39 0342 99-6379
- Website: www.livignoitaly.com

- **MADONNA DI CAMPIGLIO**
- Trento
- Italy
- Tel: +39 0465 44-2000
- E-mail: info@campiglio.net
- Website: www.campiglio.net

- **SELVA**
- Val Gardena ■ Italy
- Tel: +39 0471 79-2277
- E-mail: selva@val-gardena.com
- Website: www.val-gardena.com

SWITZERLAND

- **ADELBODEN**
- Bernese Oberland
- Switzerland
- Tel: +41 33 673-8080
- Website: www.adelboden.ch

- **ANZÈRE**
- Valais
- Switzerland
- Tel: +41 27 399-2800
- E-mail:infos@anzere.ch
- Website: www.anzere.ch

- **GSTAAD − SAANENLAND**
- Bernese Oberland
- Switzerland
- Tel: +41 33 748-8181
- Website: www.gstaad.ch

- **ANDERMATT**
- Central Switzerland
- Tel: +41 41 887-1454
- E-mail: info@andermatt.ch
- Website: www.andermatt.ch

- **ENGELBERG**
- Central Switzerland
- Tel: +41 41 637-0101
- E-mail:
tourist.center@engelberg.ch
- Website: www.engelberg.ch

- **BRAUNWALD**
- Eastern Switzerland
- Tel: +41 55 643-1108

- **DAVOS**
- Graubünden
- Switzerland
- Tel: +41 81 415-2121
- E-mail: info@davos.ch
- Website: www.davos.ch

- **ST. MORITZ**
- Graubünden ■ Switzerland
- Tel: +41 81 837-3333
- E-mail: information@stmoritz.ch
- Website: www.stmoritz.ch

- **CHATEAU D'OEX**
- Lake Geneva
- Switzerland
- Tel: +41 26 924-7788
- Website: www.chateau-doex.ch

- **VILLARS**
- Lake Geneva
- Switzerland
- Tel: +41 24 495-3232
- E-mail: information@villars.ch
- Website: www.villars.ch

- **CHAMPÈRY**
- Valais
- Switzerland
- Tel: +41 24 479-2020
- Website: www.champery.ch

- **CRANS MONTANA**
- Valais
- Switzerland
- Tel: +41 27 485-0404
- Website: www.crans-montana.ch

- **VERBIER**
- Valais
- Switzerland
- Tel: +41 27 775-3888
- E-mail: verbiertourism@verbier.ch
- Website: www.verbier.ch

- **ZERMATT**
- Valais
- Switzerland
- Tel: +41 27 967-0181
- E-mail: zermatt@wallis.ch

WIDE-OPEN RUNS AND EXCELLENT OFF-PISTE POTENTIAL MAKE DAVOS IN SWITZERLAND A WORTHY ALTERNATIVE TO NEIGHBOURING KLOSTERS RESORT.

SOUTH AMERICA

ARGENTINA

- CATEDRAL ALTA PATAGONIA
- San Carlos de Bariloche
- Argentina
- E-mail:
info@catedralaltapatagonia.com
- Website:
www.catedralaltapatagonia.com

- LAS LENAS
- San Carlos de Bariloche
- Argentina
- Tel: +54 4313 1300
- Website:
www.laslenas.com

CHILE

- FARELLONES/EL COLORADO
- Farellones ■ Chile
- Tel: +56 2 201-3704
- Website:
www.goski.com/rchi/farell.htm

- LA PARVA
- La Parva ■ Chile
- Tel: +56 2 220 9530
- Email:
parvacordillera@skilaparva.cl
- Website:
www.goski.com/rchi/parva.htm

- PORTILLO
- Portillo
- Santiago, Chile
- Tel: +56 2 361-7000
- Website:
www.skiportillo.com

AUSTRALIA

- PERISHER BLUE
- New South Wales ■ Australia
- Tel: +61 2 6459-4421
- Website:
www.perisherblue.com.au

- THREDBO
- New South Wales ■ Australia
- Tel: +61 2 6459-4100
- Website: www.thredbo.com.au

- FALLS CREEK
- Victoria ■ Australia
- Tel: +61 357 58-3224
- Website:
www.skifallscreek.com.au

- MT BULLER
- Victoria ■ Australia
- Tel: +61 357 77-6077
- Website:
www.mtbuller.com.au

- MT HOTHAM
- Victoria ■ Australia
- Tel: +61 357 59-3550
- Website:
www.mthotmham.com.au

NEW ZEALAND

WANAKA

- CARDRONA
- PO Box 117
- Wanaka
- New Zealand
- Tel: +64 3 443-7411
- E-mail: info@cardrona.com

- TREBLE CONE
- PO Box 206
- Wanaka
- Tel: +64 3 443-7443
- E-mail: info@treblecone.com
- Website: www.treblecone.com

QUEENSTOWN

- CORONET PEAK
- PO Box 359 ■ Queenstown
- Tel: +64 3 442-4620 ■ E-mail:
service@coronetpeak.co.nz
- Web: www.nzski.com/coronet

- THE REMARKABLES
- PO Box 359 ■ Queenstown
- Tel: +64 3 442-4615 ■ E-mail:
service@theremarkables.co.nz
- Website:
www.nzski.com/remarkables

JAPAN

- SHIGA KOGEN
- Nagano Province ■ Japan
- Tel: +81 269 34-2404
- Website:
www.shiakogen.gr.jp/english

- NOZAWA ONSEN
- Nagano Province ■ Japan
- Tel: +81 269 85-3166
- Website: www.vill.nozawaonsen.
nagano.jp/info/english/start.htm

Glossary

Aerial 180 To spin halfway round in the air on the snowboard, landing 'fakie' (tail end first).

Aerial 360 To spin all the way round in the air on the board, bringing the body and board full circle.

Aerial 540 To spin round in the air on the board, performing one and a half full turns of the body.

Air awareness The knowledge of how and ability to safely perform aerial manoeuvres with confidence.

Airs Jumps from the ground on a snowboard.

Alpine Downhill snowboarding involving speed and carving turns.

Avalanche transceiver A small transmitter worn in the backcountry that sends radio signals allowing rescuers to locate and rescue avalanche victims.

Avalanche Sudden fall of a large mass of snow and ice down a mountain.

Backcountry boarding Snowboarding anywhere in a wilderness area that does not form part of an established winter resort.

Boardercross A six-person race down an obstacle-laden snow track; a combination between motocross and snowboarding.

Brain bucket Jargon term for a crash helmet.

Bunny hill A gradual slope designed for skiing or snowboarding beginners.

Carving Laying out even arcs in the snow, at high speed.

Chattering (of snowboard) Vibration of a board when gliding over crud or bumps.

Corduroy Texture of a groomed run, prepared for skiers and snowboarders, which resembles the ridged fabric of the same name.

Dehydration Excessive body fluid loss (to which one may be vulnerable if not acclimatized to high mountain air). Symptoms include thirst, headache, appetite loss, nausea and dizziness.

Dropping A common warning of imminent approach to skiers or snowboarders (like the 'fore' call of golfers) used before approaching a jump.

Dual slalom Side-by-side race on parallel downhill slalom courses, where racers compete for the fastest time.

Edge angle signifies the level which a snowboard is tilted on its edge.

Fall line An imaginary line of gravity down the steepest and most direct part of a slope.

Fakie Riding with the rear foot forward.

Falling leaf Traversing by making controlled changes of direction riding alternately forwards and fakie, mimicking the action of a leaf falling from a tree.

Flex pattern The degree and location of rigidity or flexibility in a snowboard's design.

Freshies Newly dumped, untracked, virgin snow.

Frostbite Tissue damage caused by exposure to intense cold.

Garlands Consecutive turns across the fall line performed without changing edges.

Giant slalom Timed downhill race around a series of poles; with larger turns and at higher speeds than a regular slalom event.

Gondola A cable car, used to access a resort's higher elevations and more advanced terrain.

Grab Freestyle manoeuvre in which the rider holds the tail or tip of the board with his/her hand.

Halfpipe A U-shaped downhill snow trench modelled after a skateboarder's ramp of the same name, used for performing aerial freestyle manoeuvres.

Heliboarding Accessing backcountry terrain by means of a helicopter.

Hit A man-made jump, designed for aerial manoeuvres on a snowboard.

Hypothermia Drop in overall body temperature as a result of exposure to low air temperatures, to which one may be particularly vulnerable when exhausted.

Line route or path chosen by a rider.

Loading Getting onto a chairlift.

Moguls Snowy bumps made in a run by regular turns along the same path.

Off piste Any place off a marked trail, usually a good source of untracked snow.

Ollie A self-induced aerial trick performed by springing off the tail of the board.

Piste A groomed area of snow prepared for skiers and snowboarders.

Poma A tow lift that uses a small disc and pole attached to a cable; designed primarily for skiers.

Postholing Getting stuck in deep powder snow while attempting to hike.

Powder Deep dry snow which is normally freshly fallen and requires specific riding techniques.

P-tex A polyethylene plastic material used to make and repair snowboards.

Ramp Artificial or natural slope used to launch into the air.

Riding powder Surfing through soft, deep, dry powder snow.

Rope Tow A circulating loop of rope that tows the user uphill when held onto it.

Sideslip A controlled sideways slide along the fall line which allows one to bypass difficult terrain.

Slalom Timed downhill race around a series of poles at high speeds which demands balance and skill.

Snow-cat boarding Accessing backcountry terrain by means of a snow cat, an all-terrain, motorized snow transport similar to a tractor.

Stance goofy Riding the board with right foot forward.

Stance regular Riding the board with left foot forward.

Super giant slalom ('SUPER G') Downhill race with the same format as a Giant Slalom, with larger distances between gates and higher speeds.

Tail The back section of a snowboard.

T-bar A T-shaped bar attached to a cable that is designed to tow the user uphill.

Terrain park A man-made area designed for snowboarders, featuring jumps and various formations used for freestyle manoeuvres.

Thin air Air at high altitudes which is less saturated with oxygen than the air found at sea level

Trail map A map that provides important details of all the varieties of terrain at a snow resort.

Traversing Riding a snowboard diagonally across a slope's fall line.

Tree runs Off-piste runs containing tree glades and usually deeper, untracked snow.

Vitelli turns Layed-out carves or arcs in which the body stays horizontal to the snow surface; this is also known as 'Euro carves'.

Photographic Credits

Axiom/Chris Coe: pp 89, 92; Jeff Barbee: pp 9, 12 (top left), 34 (A, B), 37, 52(C), 66; John Cleare: pp 49 (background), 52 (A, B); Gallo Images/Tony Stone Images/Jess Stock: pp 35, 59; Laurence Gouault Haston: pp 4/5; INPRA/Silvio Fiore: p 48 (background); Damian Krige: pp 33 (sequence), 34 (E), 75 (sequence), 76 (sequence), 77 (sequence), 79; Marc Muench: pp 6/7; Vincent Skoglund: 8 (bottom right), 10, 56, 57, 64 (sequence), 68 (bottom left), 82; Stock Shots/Sea Hubbard: p 65; Stock Shots/R Rowland p 87; Stock Shots/Jess Stock: pp 58, 70, 90; Stock Shots/M Weyerhaeuser: p 53; Touchline/Allsport/Mike Cooper: p 67; Touchline/Allsport/Mike Powell: pp 8 (top), 11, 84; Touchline/Allsport/Anton Want: cover, p 30; David Wall: pp 2, 36, 54, 55, 62, 69, 72 (top), 73, 83.

Publishers' acknowledgements: The publishers wish to thank Vanessa Haines (PR Manager, the Ski Club of Great Britain), for her valuable input on snowboarding resorts mentioned in Chapter 7.

Thanks also to the following suppliers for their assistance and cooperation in providing clothing and equipment for photo shoots and/or permission to use existing photographs in the book — Airwalk International, Burton Snowboards, Cape Union Mart, Duotone Snowboards, F2 International/Austria, Proflex, Smileys Warehouse.

Index